KET
Testbuilder

Sarah Dymond, Nick Kenny
and Amanda French

MACMILLAN

Macmillan Education
Between Towns Road, Oxford OX4 3PP
A division of Macmillan Publishers Limited
Companies and representatives throughout the world

1 40506974 0   KET Testbuilder
1 40506976 7   KET Testbuilder with Key

First published 2005

Page make-up by eMC Design (www.emcdesign.org.uk)
Illustrated by Colin Brown (Beehive Illustration), Stephen Dew, Tony Wilkins
Cover design by Xen Media Ltd
Amanda French would like to thank Liam Keane for great support and Joe Wilson for much help and
humour.
The authors and publishers would like to thank the following for permission to reproduce their
photographs: Getty images.

Printed and bound in Great Britain by Martins the Printers Ltd.

2009 2008 2007 2006 2005
10 9 8 7 6 5 4 3 2 1

The Key English Test (KET) Testbuilder provides students with the information, advice and practice they need to pass KET. It offers teachers and students an encouraging and accessible way to prepare for the exam and may be used as part of an English language course or as a self-access programme for students preparing for the exam on their own.

There are four complete practice tests that reflect the content and level of the actual examination. All the tests are of a similar standard and include the themes, topics and vocabulary specified in the KET syllabus.

The Key English Test consists of 3 papers: Reading and Writing (9 parts); Listening (5 parts) and Speaking (2 parts). For further detail on the content of these papers, see the shaded Further Practice sections listed below.

TEST ONE

PAPER 1: READING AND WRITING   1 hour 10 minutes

Part 1

Questions 1 – 5

Which notice **(A – H)** says this **(1 – 5)**?
For questions **1 – 5**, mark the correct letter **A – H** on your answer sheet.

EXAMPLE	ANSWER
0 You can always eat here in the middle of the day.	**B**

1   You should not drive fast here.

2   You cannot take pictures here.

3   You shouldn't leave your car here.

4   You cannot use a credit card here.

5   You will pay less for things here today.

A   **OFFICE CANTEEN CASH ONLY**

B   **LUNCH SERVED Every day**

C   **VILLAGE SCHOOL SLOW DOWN**

D   **ART GALLERY Closed on Monday**

E   **MUSEUM** *No photography please*

F   **TICKET OFFICE GROUP BOOKINGS ONLY**

G   **PARKING FOR DOCTORS ONLY**

H   **SALE STARTS 08.00 TODAY**

WHAT IS TESTED

Part 1: Matching meanings to notices and signs (1 mark for each correct answer)
This tests your ability to understand notices/signs. In Part 1, you match **5 questions** to **8 notices or signs**.

ADVICE

Read questions **1 – 5** carefully because sometimes two questions may *look similar*, but the answers will have *different information*.

Sometimes a question may seem to have two different answers, but only one answer has the *right* information.

EXAMPLE A

You need to wait longer before you can <u>get on your airplane</u>.

> HEATHROW AIRPORT
> CUSTOMER INFORMATION
> Flight NZ001 – delayed 30 mins

Explanation: You need to wait longer because flight NZ001 is delayed.

You must <u>get on your airplane</u> at least 30 minutes before it leaves.

> PASSENGERS CANNOT BOARD FLIGHTS LATER
> THAN 30 MINS BEFORE DEPARTURE

Explanation: to 'board' a plane means to 'get on it'.
must get on at least 30 minutes before it leaves matches *cannot board later than 30 minutes before departure.*

EXAMPLE B

You can buy cheap theatre tickets here.

A
> TICKET OFFICE
> Half-price tickets for all afternoon shows   ✓

B
> THEATRE BOOKINGS
> Tickets for today's show only   ✗

Explanation: *cheap theatre tickets* matches *half-price tickets.* B does not say anything about the *cost* of a ticket.

PRACTICE ACTIVITIES

You can do this **before or after** you do Part 1 on page 4.

Prediction task: This helps you think about what words to look for in an answer (the notice or sign).

For each question, circle three words you think you might see in the answer (the notice). One word will probably **not** be in the answer.

Question 1 You should not drive fast here.

car   easy   slow   dangerous

Question 2 You cannot take pictures here.

allow   photography   painting   camera

Question 3 You shouldn't leave your car here.

fast   vehicle   drivers   parking

Question 4 You cannot use a credit card here.

pay   cash   buy   free

Question 5 You will pay less for things here today.

cheaper   sale   refund   price

Part 2

Questions 6 – 10

Read the sentences about going shopping.
Choose the best word **(A, B** or **C)** for each space.
For questions **6 – 10**, mark **A, B** or **C** on your answer sheet.

EXAMPLE			ANSWER
0 Akemi .... Patsy to go shopping with her.			
A talked	**B** asked	**C** decided	**B**

6   Patsy .... to the city centre by bus.
    A   moved   **B**   visited   **C**   travelled

7   Akemi and Patsy .... at the bus station.
    A   met   **B**   found   **C**   saw

8   Patsy was .... her new red coat.
    A   dressing   **B**   wearing   **C**   putting

9   Akemi wanted to buy some .... clothes for the winter.
    A   warm   **B**   sunny   **C**   hot

10   Patsy bought a new beach .... for her holiday.
    A   pillow   **B**   towel   **C**   sheet

Part 3

Questions 11 – 15

Complete the five conversations.
For questions **11 – 15**, mark **A, B** or **C** on your answer sheet.

11   Can I phone you back later?
    A   I hope so.   **B**   It's not time.   **C**   That's fine.

12   Let's have a coffee break.
    A   I do too.   **B**   That's a good idea. **C**   I'm afraid so.

13   Thank you for your help.
    A   It doesn't matter.   **B**   That's alright.   **C**   Never mind.

14   How are you?
    A   Fine thanks.   **B**   How do you do?   **C**   Don't mention it.

15   Have a nice weekend.
    A   Very well thanks.   **B**   And you.   **C**   Yes it is.

Questions 16 – 20

Complete the conversation between two friends.
What does Tina say to Adrian?

For questions **16 – 20**, mark the correct letter **A – H** on your answer sheet.

EXAMPLE		ANSWER
Adrian:	Hello Tina. How are you?	
Tina:	0	D

Adrian:	I'm fine. Did you have a good holiday in Florida?	**A**	Yes, that's right. But the other things are good too.
Tina:	16	**B**	Yes, that's true. But I enjoyed it anyway.
Adrian:	Really? Perhaps I should go there. Was it very expensive?	**C**	Well, I paid a quite lot for the flight, but the food was very cheap.
Tina:	17	**D**	Adrian! I'm very well thanks. What about you?
Adrian:	I heard that they have very good fish there.		
Tina:	18	**E**	I had a wonderful time. I'm going back again next year.
Adrian:	And did you visit any cities?	**F**	I did. But the meat is very good too.
Tina:	19		
Adrian:	Are they? I don't like swimming very much. Didn't you go to Disneyland?	**G**	Not many. I spent most of the time on the beach because the water sports are excellent.
Tina:	20		
Adrian:	Yes, you're right.	**H**	Oh yes. It's wonderful. But there are lots of other places to visit in Florida too.

Part 4

Questions 21 – 27

Read the article about a boy who crossed the Atlantic Ocean in a sailing boat.
Are sentences **21 – 27** 'Right' **(A)** or 'Wrong' **(B)**?
If there is not enough information to answer 'Right' **(A)** or 'Wrong' **(B)**, choose 'Doesn't say' **(C)**.
For questions **21 – 27**, mark **A, B** or **C** on your answer sheet.

ATLANTIC SAILOR

Sebastian Clover is a 15-year-old boy who lives in the south of England. In January, he became the youngest person ever to travel from one side of the Atlantic Ocean to the other, all alone in a sailing boat.

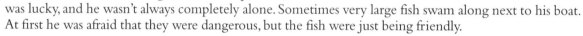

It took Sebastian 25 days to sail from Tenerife to the island of Antigua in the Caribbean. This isn't very fast, but it is a long way for someone so young!

The weather was fine during Sebastian's trip, which was lucky, and he wasn't always completely alone. Sometimes very large fish swam along next to his boat. At first he was afraid that they were dangerous, but the fish were just being friendly.

The main problem that Sebastian had on the trip was when his telephone stopped working. His parents were really worried about him, because he usually phoned them every day, but for the last three days he couldn't. Sebastian was sorry not to talk to them, but nothing else was wrong.

Sebastian kept a video diary on his trip. You will soon be able to buy this video in the shops. Sebastian wants to sail around the world next and he needs to save up some money to pay for the trip. If you buy his video, this will help him.

EXAMPLE			**ANSWER**
0 Sebastian's house is in England.			
A Right	**B** Wrong	**C** Doesn't say	**A**

---

21   Sebastian's trip started in Antigua.
   A   Right   **B**   Wrong   **C**   Doesn't say

22   Sebastian's boat travelled very quickly.
   A   Right   **B**   Wrong   **C**   Doesn't say

23   Sebastian had nice weather during the trip.
   A   Right   **B**   Wrong   **C**   Doesn't say

24   Sebastian ate a lot of fish on the trip.
   A   Right   **B**   Wrong   **C**   Doesn't say

25   Sebastian talked to his family every day on the telephone.
   A   Right   **B**   Wrong   **C**   Doesn't say

26   Sebastian made a film about his trip.
   A   Right   **B**   Wrong   **C**   Doesn't say

27   Sebastian now has enough money to sail round the world.
   A   Right   **B**   Wrong   **C**   Doesn't say

Part 5

Questions 28 – 35

Read the article about a pop singer.
Choose the best word (**A, B or C**) for each space.
For questions **28 – 35**, mark **A, B** or **C** on your answer sheet.

GWEN STEFANI

Gwen Stefani .....**0**..... born in Orange County, California .....**28**.....

October 3rd 1969. .....**29**..... are five people in Gwen's family; her

mum and dad, her sister Jill and her brothers Eric and Todd. The

family has .....**30**..... liked music and her brother started the famous

band called *No Doubt* in 1987. Gwen became the lead singer in the

band in 1988 .....**31**..... she was only 18, and she wrote one of the

band's biggest hit songs .....**32**..... is called *Hey Baby*. Eric left the

band in 1995 .....**33**..... he got a job as a cartoon artist. He now draws .....**34**..... of the pictures you see on

The Simpsons cartoon programme on television. Gwen really likes musical films and her favourite is

.....**35**..... one called *The Sound of Music*.

EXAMPLE			ANSWER
0 **A** is	**B** was	**C** has	**B**

28	**A** at	**B** on	**C** in
29	**A** Those	**B** There	**C** They
30	**A** always	**B** still	**C** yet
31	**A** so	**B** when	**C** that
32	**A** which	**B** where	**C** who
33	**A** already	**B** if	**C** because
34	**A** some	**B** much	**C** either
35	**A** this	**B** any	**C** the

WHAT IS TESTED

Part 5: Multiple-choice cloze (1 mark for each correct answer)
This tests your ability to use grammar correctly. You may be tested on prepositions, auxiliary verbs, modal verbs, pronouns, conjunctions etc.

In Part 5, you:
• read a short factual text with **8 gaps**.
• choose the correct word for each gap. You choose from **A**, **B** or **C** options.

ADVICE

Read the text first so you can have a general understanding.
Then, quickly guess the answers for each gap.
Look at the **A**, **B** or **C** options. If your guess is the same as one of the answers, you are probably correct.

It is important to read the whole sentence before you think of or choose an answer. Sometimes a word may 'fit the gap' but it doesn't fit the whole sentence.

PRACTICE ACTIVITIES

Language task

This helps you think about the right grammar word to fill the gaps.
You can do this **before or after** you do Part 5 on page 9.

Exercise 1

Choose the correct word for the gap.

is   was   has

1   "Fiona and Murray's baby .... born yesterday afternoon."

2   "Mum? I'm just calling to tell you the baby .... just been born!"

3   In the world, a baby .... born every three seconds.

at   on   in

4   "He's leaving his job .... October."

5   "The concert is .... October 25th."

6   "The party starts .... midnight."

Those   There   They

7   "Simon and Anna will be late. .... are coming by bus."

8   "I'm going to be late. .... is a big traffic jam on the motorway."

9   "I don't like these jeans. .... ones look better."

always   still   yet

10   "I've .... lived in Paris."

11   "Eric .... lives with his parents."

12   "Have you found somewhere to live ...."

so   when   that

13 Takeshi didn't know what he wanted to do .... he left school.

14 He really loved animals .... he studied to become a vet.

15 He got a job in London .... he really enjoys.

which   where   who

16 Mario went on holiday to France .... he met a woman called Claudia.

17 He fell in love with Claudia .... was very beautiful.

18 Now he's learning French .... he thinks is very difficult.

already   if   because

19 I'll only go to Germany .... I get a good job.

20 I'm going to Germany next week .... I have a new job in Berlin.

21 "Helena, can you send this report to the office in Germany?" "I've .... sent it."

some   much   either

22 Now I'm a student, I don't have .... money.

23 We're having .... problems with our new software.

24 We could .... go ski-ing or sailing.

this   any   the

25 We don't have .... food in the house!

26 Excuse me, is anyone using .... seat?

27 .... new seat I bought for my office is good for my back.

Exercise 2
Answer the questions.

Few/a few   Little/a little

We use *few/a few* with countable nouns. We use *little/a little* with uncountable nouns.

Little/few = not enough – or *– not many   a little/a few = enough –* or *– some*

Choose the best meaning for each sentence.

1 When I was studying hard at university, I had little free time.

   a   The free time I had was enough for me.   b   The free time I had wasn't enough for me.

2 We're having a few problems with the computers.

   a   We have one or two small problems.   b   We have some problems. We need to fix them.
       It doesn't matter.

3 In my opinion, there are few actors who are as good as Robert De Niro.

   a   Some actors are as good as   b   Just two or three actors are as good as
       Robert De Niro.   Robert De Niro.

4 Few people in my town speak English.

   a   So you need to learn Spanish   b   So you don't need to learn Spanish
       before you come here.   before you come here.

Dates: in/on/at

Write more examples in the gaps below.

5   **in** January, ..., ... (months)

6   **in** summer, winter, ..., ... (seasons)

7   **in** the morning, **in** the afternoon, ..., ... (general times of day)

8   **on** Monday, **on** Tuesday, ..., (days of the week)

9   **on** 1st May, **on** 6th October, ... (dates) the weekend (American English)

10   **at** Christmas, ..., ... (special holidays, religious festivals – more than 1 day)

11   **at** 2pm, **at** midnight, ... (exact times of the day)
      We also say *at night* and *at the weekend*.

A lot/much/many

We use 'a lot' in positive and negative sentences and questions forms. (countable and uncountable nouns)
We use 'many' in positive and negative sentences and question forms. (countable nouns)
We use 'much' in negative sentences and question forms. (uncountable nouns)

12   "Can I speak to you?" "Sorry, I don't have .... (or) *a lot of* time today."

13   "How .... people are there in your family?"

14   There are .... (or) .... good cafes in my town.

15   "Do you have much homework to do?" "No, not .... (or) ...."

16   "Do .... (or) .... people in your country study in a foreign university?"

17   "I don't like spicy food very ...."

18   "Do many people play basketball in your country?" "Yes, quite ...."

For/during/since

Look at the example sentences. Read the rules.

Choose the correct rule by <u>underlining</u> a word or phrase in bold.

I stayed in Hong Kong for *2 days/3 weeks/for the weekend/a year*.

EXAMPLE We use 'for' + a point/<u>a period</u> of time.

19 We *can/can't* use *for* + plural form.

20 *For* shows us the *start time to the finish time/some of the time*.

I visited Hong Kong during *my childhood/the summer/the weeks I spent travelling in Asia*.

21 We use *during* + *a point/a period of time*.

22 We *can/can't* use *during* + plural form.

23 *During* shows us *the start time to the finish time/some of the time*.

I have lived in Hong Kong since *1998/March/April 2ⁿᵈ*

24 We use *since* + *a point/a period of time*.

25 We *can/can't* use *since* + plural form.

26 *Since* is *only for past time/connects the past to the present*.

27 We use *since* with *present perfect/past simple*.

adjective/comparative adjective/superlative adjective

Complete the information below.

1 syllable adjectives	Adjectives ending in 'y'	2+ syllable adjectives
Situation: 2 people are talking about another friend.	Situation: 2 people are in a restaurant.	Situation: 2 people are looking at the prices of apartments in a newspaper.
A: "Sarah is tall, isn't she?"	A: "My curry is spicy."	A: "This apartment is expensive."
28 B: "Yes, but her brother is tall.......... than her."	**30** B: "I think this curry is spic.......... than yours."	**32** B: "Yes, but this apartment is .... expensive than that one!"
29 A: "I know! Her brother is the tall.......... person I've ever met!"	**31** A: "I don't think so. This curry is the .... one on the menu!"	**33** A: "And this one with a swimming pool is the .... expensive apartment I've seen!"

What are the different adjective forms for?

34 good ....   **35** bad ....

Part 6

Questions 36 – 40

Read the descriptions of things you find in a restaurant.
What is the word for each one?
The first letter is already there. There is one space for each other letter in the word.

For questions **36 – 40**, write the words on your answer sheet.

EXAMPLE	ANSWER
0 Customers in a restaurant sit on one of these.	c h a i r

36   This man brings you your food.   w _ _ _ _ _

37   This tells you what you can eat at the restaurant.   m _ _ _

38   This tells you how much to pay after your meal.   b _ _ _

39   Your food is cooked here.   k _ _ _ _ _ _

40   You use this to cut food.   k _ _ _ _

Part 7

Questions 41 – 50

Complete these emails.
Write ONE word for each space.
For questions **41 – 50**, write the words on the answer sheet.

To: The Manager, Nelson Hotel, Stamford
From: Lucy Morton
Re: Lost property

Dear Sir,

Last weekend I stayed (**Example** .in.) Room 133 at your hotel ......**41**.... three nights from Friday ......**42**.... Monday. I think ......**43**.... left a cassette in the cupboard next to the bed. It belongs ......**44**.... my teacher at the Oxford English School ......**45**.... let me borrow it for a few days.

Please ......**46**.... you look for ......**47**.... for me ?

Thank you

Lucy Morton

To: Lucy Morton
From: W. Fisher
Re: Lost property

Dear Ms Morton,

We think we have found ......**48**.... cassette. ......**49**.... it called *Listen to English*? Can you come and get it, ...**50**.... shall we post it to you?

Yours sincerely

W. Fisher
Manager
Nelson Hotel

Part 8

Questions 51 – 55

Read the information about CDs and the note to Graham.
Complete the customer order form.
For questions **51 – 55**, write the information on your answer sheet.

Music CDs at special prices:	
Brazilian Disco Music	£4.99
Italian Love Songs	£5.99
German Piano Concert	£2.99

Order from:
Ace Music Shop
24 Blake Drive
London

Carrington Computers
16 West Road
Cambridge

12 March

Graham,

Can you order me a disc with your credit card, please?
I need some dance music for the office party next week.
I'll pay you back.

Thanks

Emma Parks

Customer Order Form

Customer:	*Emma Parks*
Address:	**51**
Name of CD:	**52**
Price:	**53** £
Date of Order:	**54**
Pay with:	**55**

Part 9

Question 56

Read this email from your English penfriend, Chris.

> Here is a picture of my house. How big is your house? What is your room like? What is the best thing about your house?
>
> Chris

Write Chris an email. Answer the questions.
Write **25 – 35** words.
Write the email on your answer sheet.

WHAT IS TESTED

Part 9: Writing (5 marks)
Part 9 tests your ability to write a short message, a note or a postcard.

You <u>first</u> need to read
either a short message/a note/a postcard
or some instructions.

You <u>then</u> need to write your answer.
There are always **3** things you need to include in the answer.
You need to write between **25 – 35** words.

ADVICE

1 Find the **3** things you need to include in your answer. You <u>must</u> write about all **3** things.

2 Do not write fewer than **25** words.

3 Start and finish your answer correctly.

EXAMPLE

Dear Chris   from Linda

4 It's OK to make small grammar and spelling errors. The most important thing is that you include the **3** things in your answer and that you can write about them clearly enough for a reader to understand.

PRACTICE ACTIVITIES

You can do this **before or after** you do Part 9 on page 15.

Exercise 1: Writing about the 3 things: Here are two answers **A** and **B** to question 56 on page 15. Both answers are good because they include the **3** things that Chris asks about and the meaning is clear.

Read **A** and **B** and find the sentences which answer the questions.

1 How big is your house?
2 What is your room like?
3 What is the best thing about your house?

A
Dear Chris
I live in a small apartement with my family. I am share a room with my brother so it's a bit untidy. I love that our apartement has a nice balcony where I sit in the sun.

Mario

B
Dear Chris
The best thing of my house is the view – everywhere there are mountain. It's quite large so if you come in Japan, you can stay with us.

My room is full of university books! I have to study hard!

Love Michiko

Exercise 2: Find the mistakes in **A** and **B**.

A spelling mistake = ...   grammar mistake = ...

B 2 preposition mistakes = ...   a mistake with a plural form = ...

Exercise 3: In Part 9, you may have to describe something or someone.

a Read the questions below. What are they asking about?

What do you look like?	personality/appearance/interests?
What are you like?	personality/appearance/interests?
What do you like?	personality/appearance/interests?

b Read the questions below. Circle the answers which are correct.

1 What does your friend look like?

She has		is	
She is	dark hair and she	looks like	quite tall.
She looks like			

2 What is your friend like?

She has		has	
She is	friendly and she	is	really funny.
She likes		likes	

3 What does your friend like?

	playing tennis	
She likes	to play tennis	at weekends.
	play tennis	

Exercise 4: Use all of the adjectives in the box to complete the description below.

new   retired   dark   different   younger   quiet   tall   small   intelligent

I have a **(1)** .... family. There are only four of us: my mother and father, my **(2)** .... sister and me. My father used to be a doctor, but now he's **(3)** .... Nowadays he likes playing golf and he's also learning Japanese. My mother still works. She's a journalist for a newspaper. My sister is like my mother. They're both very **(4)** .... and they look like each other. Both of them are **(5)** .... and blonde. I look more like my father - we have **(6)** .... hair and the same colour eyes. But my dad is a **(7)** .... person, but I like going out to parties and meeting **(8)** .... people. The members of my family are quite **(9)** ...., but we get on very well.

TEST ONE

PAPER 2: LISTENING (30 minutes)

Part 1

Questions 1 – 5

You will hear five short conversations.
You will hear each conversation twice.
There is one question for each conversation.
For questions **1 – 5**, put a tick **(✓)** under the right answer.

EXAMPLE

0   How many people were at the party?

20	**30**	**50**
A ☐	B ✓	C ☐

1   What time is the girl's appointment?

  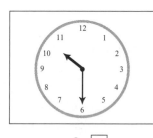

A ☐   B ☐   C ☐

2   How far is the nearest petrol station?

2 kms   4 kms   10 kms

A ☐   B ☐   C ☐

3   What did Monica do at the weekend?

A ☐   **B** ☐   **C** ☐

4   Which fruit does the woman buy?

      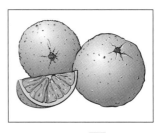

A ☐   **B** ☐   **C** ☐

5   Where is the man going next year?

| **China** | **Japan** | **Thailand** |

A ☐   **B** ☐   **C** ☐

WHAT IS TESTED

Part 1: Three-option multiple choice (1 mark for each correct answer)

This tests your ability to understand the most important information in a conversation. You may need to listen for information such as: prices, days of the week, numbers, times, countries, shapes etc.

In Part 1, you need to choose the correct answer for **5 questions**. Each question has **3 answers** but only **1 answer** is correct.

For all parts of the Listening paper, you hear everything twice.

ADVICE

For this part, you need to read each question very carefully. When you listen to a conversation, you may hear the speakers talk about **all 3 answers**, but only **1 answer** will match the question.

EXAMPLE   What time will Mary's train arrive in Weston?

3.00	3.15	3.30
A	B	C

Man:	When does your train leave, Mary?
Woman:	At 3.15, but I want to be there at 3.00.
Man:	How long does it take to get to Weston?
Woman:	Oh, I should be there at 3.30.

Answer = C

Explanation

The speakers mention all 3 times, but the question asks when the train will **arrive** in Weston. 3pm is when Mary wants to arrive at her local station. 3.15pm is when Mary's train arrives at the local station. 3.30pm is when the train arrives at Weston, the place where Mary wants to travel to.

PRACTICE ACTIVITIES

You should do this **after** you do Part 1 on pages 18 and 19.

Understanding spoken English

Spoken English can be difficult to understand because English speakers:

- use a lot of pronouns

EXAMPLE: "Did you speak to Julie?"   "Yes, I spoke to **her** this morning."
                 "Have you written your report?"   "Yes, I wrote **it** last night."

- use different words instead of repeating the same word

EXAMPLE: " Have you been to that new Mexican restaurant yet?"   "Yes, I went **there** last week."
                 "Can I borrow your dictionary?"   "Sorry, I don't have **one**."

- use short forms to answer questions

EXAMPLE: "Do you speak another language?"   "Yes, I **do**." (speak another language)
                 "Would you like to go to the beach with us?"   "Yes, I **would**." (like to go to the beach with you)

Now read the listening script for each conversation and answer the questions below.

Question 1: What time is the girl's appointment?

Boy:	*Are you going to the dentist's in the morning?*
Girl:	*Yes. I wanted to go at nine-thirty, but (1) they (2) only had appointments at either ten o'clock or ten-thirty. (3)*
Boy:	*But your class starts at ten-thirty.*
Girl:	*I know. So I'm going at ten. (4) But it (5) should be OK.*

1   What time did the girl first want to have an appointment?
2   Who or what is 'they'?
3   What two possible appointment times did the dentist offer the girl?
4   Why does the girl not want a 10.30 appointment?

5　What does 'It should be OK' mean?

　　a　I know the dentist. He's good at his job.

　　b　I don't have problems with my teeth.

　　c　I will have enough time to travel from the dentist's to my class.

Question 2: How far is the nearest petrol station?

Woman:　*Excuse me, is Wellstown far from here?*

Man:　*It's **(1)** about 10 kilometres away.*

Woman:　*Is there a petrol station on the way? **(2)***

Man:　*There's one **(3)** about 2 kilometres down this road on the left and another **(4)** 4 kilometres away on the main road.*

1　What does 'It' mean?

2　What does 'on the way' mean?

3　What does 'one' mean?

4　What does 'another' mean?

5　What is 2 km away?　　What is 4km away?　　What is 10km away?

Question 3: What did Monica do at the weekend?

Boy:　*Hi Monica. Did you have a good time cycling at the weekend?**(1)***

Monica:　*Well, I didn't go cycling in the end. **(2)** My friend has just bought a new sports car, so we went out in that. **(3)***

Boy:　*Really? That **(4)** sounds fun.*

Monica:　*Yes, it **(5)** was just like the one **(6)** in the advertisement on television.*

1　Why does the boy ask this question?

　　a　Before the weekend, Monica told him she planned to go cycling.

　　b　After the weekend, Monica told him she went cycling.

2　What does 'in the end' tell us in this sentence?

　　a　Monica went cycling only on Saturday.

　　b　Monica changed her plans.

3　What does 'that' mean?

4　What does 'that' mean?

5　What does 'it' mean?

6　What does 'the one' mean?

Question 4: Which fruit does the woman buy?

Woman:　*I'd like to buy some fruit, please? Have you got any bananas?*

Man:　*Sorry. I've got some very nice apples or some oranges, but I've sold all my bananas.*

Woman:　*It's OK, oranges will be fine. One kilo please. I've already got some apples at home.*

Man:　*Thank you.*

1　What does 'Sorry' mean?　**a** Yes, I have got some bananas.　**b** No, I haven't got any bananas.

2　Does the man have bananas for sale now?　**a** Yes　**b** No

3　What does 'oranges will be fine' mean?　**a** I want to buy oranges.　**b** I don't want to buy oranges.

4　The woman wants a kilo of ....?

5　The woman doesn't buy any apples because　**a** she doesn't like them.　**b** she has apples at home.

Question 5: Where is the man going next year? (1)

Woman:　And do you have to travel **(2)** to other countries as part of your job?

Man:　Yes. I went **(3)** to China last month and next year I'm going **(4)** to Japan.

Woman:　Oh you are lucky. And have you been **(5)** to Thailand yet?

Man:　Oh yes. I've been **(6)** three times actually.

Match **1 – 6** (a grammatical structure) with

　　　　a (present time: routines and habits)

　　　　b (future plans)

　　　　c (past time – when we know exactly when something happened)

　　　　d (past time – to talk about someone's experience + when the exact time is not important)

　　　　EXAMPLE: 1 = **b**

Part 2

Questions 6 – 10

Listen to David telling Tina about his new flat.
Which person gave him each thing in the flat?
For questions **6 – 10**, write a letter **(A – H)** next to each person.
You will hear the conversation twice.

EXAMPLE	**ANSWER**
0 Father	**B**

People

6   brother   ☐

7   sister   ☐

8   grandfather   ☐

9   grandmother   ☐

10   mother   ☐

Gift

A   chairs

B   CD player

C   desk

D   lamp

E   mirror

F   shelves

G   sofa

H   table

WHAT IS TESTED

Part 2: Matching (1 mark for each correct answer)

This tests your ability to match the information in **2 lists**.

There are **5 items** in the first list. There are **8 items** to choose from in the second list.

EXAMPLE: you match: 5 people to 5 hobbies
5 days to 5 classes
5 places to 5 activities

ADVICE

In Part 2, you often hear the speakers talk about all **8 items** in the second list. Only **5 items** match the first list. **3 items** do not match the first list.

You hear the recording twice. When you listen for the second time, check that you chose the correct information in the second list.

PRACTICE ACTIVITIES

You should do this **after** you do Part 2 on page 22.

1   Listening and pronunciation task

English speakers put stress on: nouns, verbs, adjectives and adverbs (information or content words)

English speakers usually don't put stress on: auxiliary verbs, pronouns, prepositions, articles, conjunctions.

When you listen to an English speaker, you can hear the information/content words more easily than the other words.

When you do the Listening paper, you <u>do not need</u> to understand every word. It is more important to hear the information/content words.

Read the listening script for Part 2 below.

<u>Underline</u> the words which have the strongest stress.

EXAMPLE

Tina: Thanks David – What a <u>beautiful</u> flat! <u>Where</u> did you <u>get</u> all these <u>things</u>?

David: Well, my <u>father</u> <u>bought</u> the <u>CD player</u> …

… and the other things were presents from my family too. My brother gave me that red sofa. It was in his flat with two red chairs, but it was too big. He's still got the chairs.

Tina: And what about the table that the CD player's on?

David: My sister gave me that. She bought a new table and chairs when she got married.
This is her old one.

Tina: And this desk looks really old.

David: Yeah, it was my grandfather's desk when he was a student. He gave me that and my grandmother gave me that mirror over there on the wall next to the lamp.

Tina: And what about your mother?

David: She bought me those bookshelves. My brother helped me put them on the wall.
We put the mirror up at the same time.

Tina: It all looks really nice.

Listen to the recording again and check your answers.

Part 3

Questions 11 – 15

Listen to Gary asking about a video shop.

For questions **11 – 15**, tick (✓) **A**, **B** or **C**.

You will hear the conversation twice.

EXAMPLE	ANSWER
0 The video shop is	
A near a bus station.	☐
B next to a train station.	✔
C opposite a petrol station.	☐

11 Each video costs

    A £1.50 per day. ☐

    B £2.00 per day. ☐

    C £5.00 per day. ☐

12 The video club has a meeting

    A once a week. ☐

    B once a month. ☐

    C once a year. ☐

13 Most of the video shop's films are

    A American. ☐

    B Australian. ☐

    C British. ☐

14 On Saturday, the shop closes at

    A seven o'clock. ☐

    B eight o'clock. ☐

    C twelve o'clock. ☐

15 Gary will get a form

    A by post. ☐

    B from the shop. ☐

    C on the club's website. ☐

Part 4

Questions 16 – 20

You will hear a conversation at a college.
Listen and complete the questions **16 – 20**.
You will hear the information twice.

COLLEGE COURSE

First name:	GAVIN
Surname:	**16**
Name of course:	**17**
Date the course starts:	**18**
Day of Course:	**19**
Cost of one lesson:	**20** £

Part 5

Questions 21 – 25

You will hear some information about a supermarket.

Listen and complete questions **21 – 25**.
You will hear the information twice.

NEWMAN'S SUPERMARKET

SPECIAL THINGS TODAY:

Free book:	**21** *When you buy ....*
Special Price:	**22** *£ .... for 100 grams of chocolate*
In the Restaurant today:	**23** *Sandwiches or .... soup*
Competition:	**24** *Win a ....*
	25 *Put your name and .... on a card.*

You now have eight minutes to write your answers on the answer sheet.

TEST ONE

PAPER 3: SPEAKING (8 – 10 minutes)

Part 1 (5-6 minutes)

Here are some questions that you might hear in the Speaking paper.

What's your name?

How do you spell your surname?

Where do you live?

Do you like living there? Why/Why not?

What do you do in your free time?

Do you often watch television? Why/Why not?

Tell me about the type of television programmes you like.

If you are in class, work with a partner.

Student A: Ask the questions.

Student B: Listen and answer the questions.

Now change roles.

Student B: Ask the questions.

Student A: Listen and answer the questions.

If you are working alone, you can answer the questions and record yourself.

When you play the cassette, listen and think about what you said:

•   did you know all the vocabulary you needed?

•   did you use the right tenses?

•   do you think your pronunciation of words was clear?

WHAT IS TESTED

Part 1: Giving personal information

This tests your ability to understand and answer questions about you.

The questions might ask about: your occupation, your studies, your family, your hometown, your free time, your interests, your plans etc

You may need to talk about the past, present and future.

In the Speaking paper, there are:
- 2 or sometimes 3 'candidates'. (people taking the test)
- 2 examiners. One examiner is the 'interlocutor'. This person asks you the questions. The other examiner is the 'assessor'. This person only listens and makes notes. Both examiners decide what marks you receive.

In Part 1, you only speak to the 'interlocutor'. You do not need to speak to the other candidate.

ADVICE

1   The examiners are listening for three things:
- Your grammar and vocabulary
- Your pronunciation
- Your interactive communication skills

Grammar and Vocabulary

Your grammar does not need to be correct all the time. You do not need to know all the vocabulary for everything you want to say. The most important thing is that you are able to communicate your message.

Your pronunciation

This does not need to be perfect. The most important thing is that it is clear enough for the listener to understand.

Your interactive communication skills

This is your ability to communicate naturally with the examiner or the other candidate. It includes:
- asking the examiner or candidate to repeat something
- explaining something in a different way if the other person doesn't understand
- responding to something the other person said

2   In Part 1 of the Speaking paper,
you should:
- be able to spell your name
- give longer answers sometimes
- correct your mistakes – if you can do it quickly

you can:
- ask the examiner to repeat the question if you didn't understand .
- hesitate <u>a little</u> (" I think, er, that Athens is an interesting city.")

you shouldn't:
- give too many short answers
- worry about every mistake
- hesitate <u>too much</u> (I think, er, I think, er, Athens, er…etc)

PRACTICE ACTIVITIES

You can do this **before or after** you do Part 1 on page 26.

Look at the three conversations below. Which conversation is (A) very good (B) good (C) not good? Why?

Conversation 1	Conversation 2	Conversation 3
Examiner: What's your name?	**Examiner:** What's your name?	**Examiner:** What's your name?
Candidate: Sara Buehler	**Candidate:** Marc Achermann	**Candidate:** Peter Schlatter
Examiner: Where do you come from, Sara?	**Examiner:** How do you spell your surname?	**Examiner:** Where do you live, Peter?
Candidate: I'm from Switzerland, from the capital, Berne.	**Candidate:** A-C-H-E-R-M-A-N-N	**Candidate:** I'm from Berne, in Switzerland.
Examiner: Oh, yes? Do you like living there?	**Examiner:** Thank you. Where do you live, Marc?	**Examiner:** Do you like living there?
Candidate: It's OK. It's a bit, er, expensive but there are lots of shops.	**Candidate:** Switzerland.	**Candidate:** It's, er, not so bad. There are many peoples, I mean, people, in Berne. It has villages in Switzerland – not many people – so it's bored, er, boring.
Examiner: What do you do in your free time?	**Examiner:** What town or city do you come from in Switzerland?	
Candidate: Well, I go usually shopping with my sister, I play basketball, I go ski-ing in the winter.	**Candidate:** Berne.	**Examiner:** I see. What do you do in your free time?
	Examiner: Do you like living there?	
Examiner: Do you often watch television?	**Candidate:** Yes.	**Candidate:** I like the computer games and er, I don't know the English word, er, you make ski-ing not in the mountains – you make it on the countryside.
	Examiner: Why?	
Candidate: Sometimes. Maybe I watch it for 4 hours, maybe 5 hours a week.	**Candidate:** I like there, Berne.	
	Examiner: What do you do in your free time?	**Examiner:** Cross-country ski-ing. I see. Do you often watch television?
Examiner: Tell me about the type of television programmes you like.	**Candidate:** I playing guitar. Listen music.	
	Examiner: Do you often watch television?	**Candidate:** Sorry – can you repeat that, please?
Candidate: I prefer, er, serious programmes like the news, or some informations programmes.	**Candidate:** Yes, I watch.	**Examiner:** Yes. Do you often watch television programmes?
	Examiner: Tell me about the type of television programmes you like.	
	Candidate: I watch on weekends television.	

You could now do the Speaking paper on page 26 again.

Part 2 (A)   **(3-4 minutes)**

Candidate A, here is some information about a hotel.

LONDON HOTEL

       Green Avenue

       More than 50 rooms

       Each with its own bathroom

       Excellent restaurant

Prices: $100 single room

          $150 double room

Candidate B, you don't know anything about the hotel, so ask **A** some questions about it.

Candidate B – your questions

HOTEL

what/name?

many rooms?

private bathroom?

dinner?

price/room?

Part 2 (B)

Now **Candidate B**, it's your turn to have some information.

Candidate B, here is some information about a sports centre.

CITY SPORTS CENTRE

everyday – tennis, swimming and horse-riding
weekends only – football and basketball

coffee bar with snacks

Prices: £50 per year (adults)
           £35 per year (students)

Candidate A, you don't know anything about the sports centre, so ask **B** some questions about it.

Now **A** asks questions about the sports centre and **B** answers them.

Candidate A – your questions

SPORTS CENTRE

what/name?

tennis?

when?

eat/drink?

student price?

WHAT IS TESTED

Part 2: Prompt card activity
This tests your ability to understand and ask questions about factual information.

* You read some information on a card.
* Your partner uses 5 questions on another card to ask you about the information you have.
* You answer your partner's questions.

This is repeated with different cards. Your partner has the information and you ask the questions.

In Part 2 of the Speaking paper, you only speak to your partner. You do not speak to the examiners.

ADVICE

In Part 2 of the Speaking paper you should:
* look at your partner, not the examiner
* listen to your partner's questions and give a 'full' answer

EXAMPLE: *"What time does the museum open?"*

"It opens at 7 am, from Monday to Friday." ✓

"7am. Monday to Friday." ✗

* listen to your partner's answers and respond in a natural way

EXAMPLE: *"It costs $10 for adults and $5 for children."*
"<u>I see. That's good</u>. And what time does …?" etc ✓
"What time does …?" ✗
correct your mistakes – if you can, do it quickly

you can:
* ask the examiner to repeat the question
* ask your partner to repeat the question

you shouldn't:
* worry about every grammar mistake
* worry if you think your partner is better or worse than you. (The examiners give you separate marks and the important thing is that you communicate with your partner.)

PRACTICE ACTIVITIES

You can do this **before or after** you do Part 2 on page 29.

Look at the questions about the hotel and the sports centre on pages 29 and 30.
Exercise 1: Write the questions in full.

EXAMPLE   <u>HOTEL</u>
              what/name? = What's the name of the hotel?

Now read the dialogue between two candidates, Roberto and Sylvia, below. Are your questions the same?

Examiner: Roberto, here is some information about a hotel. Sylvia, you don't know anything about the hotel, so ask Roberto some questions about it. Now, Sylvia, ask Roberto your questions about the hotel and Roberto, you answer them.

Sylvia: Roberto, what's the name of the hotel?
Roberto: It's called the London Hotel.
Sylvia: OK, The London Hotel, and how many rooms does it have?
Roberto: More than 50 rooms – it's quite large.
Sylvia: Really? And can I have a private bathroom?
Roberto: Er … yes, each room has its own bathroom. You can have a private bathroom.
Sylvia: Great. What about dinner? Can I have dinner in this hotel?
Roberto: Yes, it has an excellent restaurant. You can eat here.
Sylvia: Good. How much does a room cost?
Roberto: It costs $100 for a single room and $150 for a double room.
Sylvia: I see. Thank you.

Examiner: Thank you. Right, Sylvia, here is some information about a sports centre. Roberto, you don't know anything about the sports centre, so ask Sylvia some questions about it. Now Roberto, ask Sylvia your questions about the sports centre and Sylvia, you answer them.

Roberto: OK, Sylvia, what's the name of the sports centre?
Sylvia: It's, er, the City Sports Centre.
Roberto: OK. Can I play tennis in this sports centre?
Sylvia: Yes, you can. And also you can go swimming and horse-riding.
Roberto: That's good. When can I play tennis?
Sylvia: Everyday, if you want.
Roberto: Right, and can I eat and drink something at the sports centre?
Sylvia: Yes, there is a coffee bar with snacks. You can get something here.
Roberto: That's great, and, er, I'm a student. Is there a cheaper price for a student, for this sports club?
Sylvia: Yes, the cost is £50 per year but for you, for students, it's £35 a year, OK?
Roberto: OK. Very good.

Examiner: Thank you very much. That's the end of the test.

Exercise 2: Read the dialogue again. <u>Underline</u> the words or phrases that Roberto and Sylvia use to show they are listening to the answers.

EXAMPLE

Roberto: It's called the London Hotel.
Sylvia: <u>OK, the London Hotel</u>, and how many rooms does it have?

Exercise 3: Read the questions below. In each group, which 2 questions are correct? Which one has a mistake? Can you correct them?

HOTEL

a   *what/name?*

What's the name of the hotel? How is the hotel called? What's the hotel called?

....

....

b   *many rooms?*

Does it have many rooms? How many rooms does it have? There are many rooms here?

....

....

c   *private bathroom?*

Does it have an own bathroom? Do the rooms have their own bathroom? Can I have a private bathroom?

....

....

d   *dinner?*

Can I have dinner in this hotel? Is it possible to have dinner here? Is there a dinner here?

....

....

e   *price/room?*

How much does a room cost? How much does it cost a room? What is the price of a room?

....

....

SPORTS CENTRE

f   *tennis?*

Is it possible to play tennis here? It has tennis at the sports centre? Can I play tennis in this sports centre?

....

....

g   *when?*

What times can I play tennis? How often can I play tennis here? When can I play tennis?

....

....

h   *eat/drink?*

Can I eat and drink something here? Is it possible to eat and drink something here? There is anything to eat and drink here?

....

....

i   *student price?*

Is it possible a student price? Is there a cheaper price for a student? How much do students pay?

....

....

TEST TWO

PAPER 1: READING AND WRITING (1 hour 10 minutes)

Part 1

Questions 1 – 5

Which notice **(A – H)** says this **(1 – 5)**?
For questions **1 – 5**, mark the correct letter **A – H** on your answer sheet.

EXAMPLE	ANSWER
0 We can tell you about places to visit.	**F**

1   We may have the bag you lost.

A   SALE STARTS HERE NEXT WEEK

2   You can come here six days a week.

B   Take a seat until your name is called

3   You can always buy things cheaply here.

C   Left Luggage Office

4   Please wait here.

D   Swimming Pool
Open Mon-Sat 10.00–21.00

5   We will be here later this afternoon.

E   College open to Visitors
Tues–Sat afternoons only

F   Tourist Information Office

G   Berry's Leather Handbags
Lowest prices in town

H   Closed for Lunch
Back at 3.00 pm

PRACTICE ACTIVITIES

You can do this **before or after** you do Part 1 on page 34.

Language task: This helps you think about the grammar in questions **1 – 5**.

In Part 1, you can often see the modal verbs '**can/cannot, must/mustn't, should/shouldn't/have to/may**' in questions **1 – 5**.

Exercise 1: Read the exercise below and write a modal verb in the right gap.

a   You .... be late if the bus doesn't arrive soon!

b   Sorry, you .... (or) .... smoke inside this office.

c   You .... go to that restaurant. It's not very good.

d   After you finish the test, you .... (or) ....leave if you want to.

e   You .... (or) .... show your passport at the check-in desk.

f   We .... go swimming today because the pool is closed!

g   I think you .... see a doctor if you are ill.

Exercise 2: Choose a phrase from the box to replace the modal verbs. Write the correct phrase in the right gap.

it is necessary to	it's not a good idea to	you are allowed to	it's possible that you will
you are not allowed to	it's not possible to	it's a good idea to	

a   .... be late if the bus doesn't arrive soon.

b   Sorry, ... smoke inside this office.

c   .... go to that restaurant. It's not very good.

d   After you finish the test, ... leave if you want to.

e   .... show your passport at the check-in desk.

f   .... go swimming today because the pool is closed.

g   .... see a doctor if you are ill.

Language check

Have to + must

English-speakers use *have* to and *must* to speak about <u>what is necessary</u>.

"I have to get a visa for my holiday in the USA." = It is necessary for me to get a visa because that is <u>the law</u> in the USA.

EXAMPLE *"My boss says I have to finish my report today."* = It's not possible to finish the report tomorrow. I have <u>an order</u> from my boss.

EXAMPLE *"I must send an email to Chris today. It's his birthday!"* = It is necessary for me to send an email to Chris <u>because it's his birthday</u>.

EXAMPLE *"I must get a haircut today. I have a job interview tomorrow!"* = It is necessary for me to have a haircut <u>because I want to look good in my interview</u>.

There is not much difference between *have to* and *must*. We often use *have to* when there is a law or a rule or an order from <u>another person</u>. We often use *must* when <u>we</u> think something is important or necessary.

Mustn't = you are not allowed to

EXAMPLE: *"You must not swim between the two red flags."* = This is the rule on the beach.

Don't have to = you don't need to

EXAMPLE: *"I love weekends because I don't have to get up early! I can stay in bed all morning!"* = I don't need to get up early because I don't go to work at weekends. I can choose to get up early or I can choose to stay in bed.

Exercise 3: Write a sentence for each notice. Use a modal verb in your sentence. The first one is done as an example.

NO PARKING	You .... *can't* .... park here.
No cheques or credit cards	You .... pay with cash.
GOLF CLUB: Members only	Only members .... play here.
Motorway: Expect delays this weekend	Drivers .... start their journey early.
Do not walk on the grass	You .... walk on the grass.
Play area: Children over three only	Children under three .... play here.
Warning: Lock your car!	Drivers .... forget to lock their cars.
No parking between 9am – 5pm	You .... park here after 5pm and before 9pm.
Cheap fares for students	Students .... buy cheap fares here.
Book now! Tickets selling fast!	You .... buy tickets now.
Museum shop: *Closed for lunch*	Customers .... come back after lunch.
Film not suitable for young children	Young children .... watch this film.

Part 2

Questions 6 – 10

Read the sentences about a day trip.
Choose the best word (**A, B** or **C**) for each space.
For questions **6 – 10**, mark **A, B** or **C** on your answer sheet.

EXAMPLE			ANSWER
0 Charles and Tanya decided to .... a day in a big city.			
A pass	**B** spend	**C** take	**B**

6   They wanted to see some important buildings and .... some famous museums.
   A   visit   **B**   go   **C**   stay

7   It .... them three hours to get to the city by coach.
   A   made   **B**   took   **C**   had

8   They felt .... when they arrived, so they went to a coffee shop.
   A   thirsty   **B**   angry   **C**   noisy

9   They bought a map to help them find their .... around the city.
   A   road   **B**   street   **C**   way

10   They .... some postcards to their parents and friends.
   A   sent   **B**   bought   **C**   looked

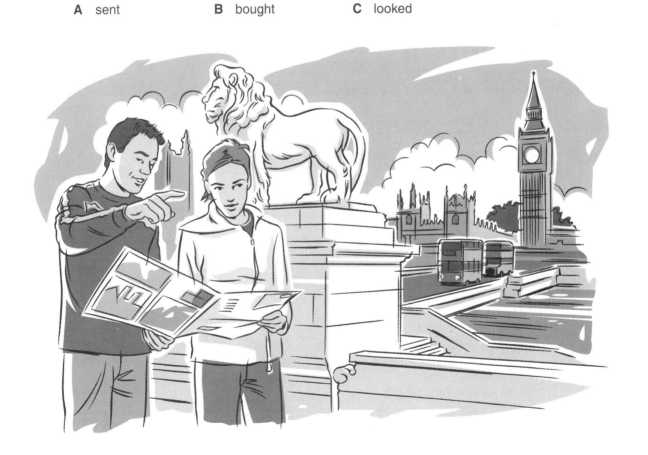

WHAT IS TESTED

Part 2: 3-option multiple-choice gap fill (1 mark for each correct answer)
This tests your ability to understand and use vocabulary.

In Part 2:
- you read six sentences. The six sentences are part of a story or one topic.
- each sentence has a gap
- you choose one of three words to fill the gap
- the 3 words are all verbs or all nouns or all adjectives

ADVICE

Read the instructions at the top of the page. This helps you understand the <u>situation</u> or <u>topic</u>.
EXAMPLE: *Read the sentences about <u>a day trip</u>.*

When you are choosing a verb, ask yourself:
- does this verb need a preposition? what preposition?
EXAMPLE: *I'm <u>going to</u> the supermarket later.*

- does this verb need an object or a pronoun after?
EXAMPLE: *Maria <u>told</u> <u>Bruno</u> about the party.*

- does this verb need an 'ing' form or an infinitive after?
EXAMPLE: *Wei-ping <u>practises</u> <u>playing</u> the violin every day.*

When you are choosing an adjective, ask yourself:
- which noun does the adjective describe?
EXAMPLE: *The students finished* **the test** *quickly because* **it** *was* ....
clever   easy   hard-working

PRACTICE ACTIVITIES

You can do this **before or after** you do Part 2 on page 37.

Language task

Exercise 1: This helps you think about <u>how</u> to choose the correct answer.

Choose a verb that goes with all 3 nouns/phrases below.

pass   spend   take
1 .... a trip/a photo/a bus
2 .... time/money/a day doing something
3 .... an exam/a test/the time

visit   go   stay
4 .... a museum/my relatives/Paris
5 .... at home/with my friends/in Paris
6 .... back home/to my house/to Paris

make   take   have
7 .... a party/a large family/a problem
8 .... a holiday/a taxi/a walk
9 .... a noise/a film/dinner

send   buy   look
10 .... a new car/dollars/food
11 .... a letter to someone/a fax/information
12 .... at a letter from someone/at the view/happy

Choose the correct adjective.

thirsty   angry   noisy

13   My younger brother was .... <u>because</u> he <u>didn't want to go to bed</u>.

14   My younger brother was .... <u>so</u> I asked him to <u>play somewhere else</u>.

15   My younger brother was .... <u>so</u> I gave him <u>a drink</u>.

Choose the correct noun.

road   street   way

16   "Excuse me, can you tell me the .... to the library?"

17   You should drive slowly on a countryside ....

18   "I'm sorry I'm late. I lost my ....?"

19   "The bank is on the high ...., at the end of all the shops."

20   "We live on a busy .... / ....".

Exercise 2: The infinitive or -*ing* form?

Finish the sentence by writing the correct form of the word in brackets.

a   I <u>spend</u> a lot of time .... (take) photographs.

b   My mother <u>made</u> me .... (eat) a lot of vegetables when I was a child.

c   I wasn't <u>allowed</u> .... (eat) any chocolate and she didn't let me .... (eat) any junk food either.

d   I <u>enjoy</u> .... (meet) my friends and .... (go) out for coffee.

e   I have <u>decided</u> .... (find) a new job next year.

f   Please <u>remember</u> .... (call) Mr Kim this afternoon.

g   You must <u>practice</u> .... (use) chopsticks if you want to live in Japan.

h   I <u>would like</u> .... (visit) Australia next year.

i   I'm <u>interested in</u> .... (travel) and .... (see) different cultures.

j   I <u>hate</u> .... (drive) in the city. There's so much traffic!

k   I <u>apologize for</u> .... (be) late.

Part 3

Questions 11 – 15

Complete the five conversations.

For questions **11 – 15**, mark **A, B** or **C** on your answer sheet.

11 How is your mother?

   A Fine thanks.   **B** With my father.   **C** Forty-four.

12 Tom, this is my wife, Penny.

   A Who are you?   **B** Pleased to meet you.   **C** Don't mention it.

13 When can we go shopping?

   A I'm afraid not.   **B** Any time you like.   **C** That will be nice.

14 Let's have a cup of coffee.

   A I do too.   **B** I hope so.   **C** That's a good idea.

15 Do you like jazz music?

   A Not very much.   **B** It doesn't matter.   **C** Oh good!

Questions 16 – 20

Complete the conversation between two friends.
What does Jason say to Miranda?

For questions **16 – 20**, mark the correct letter **A – H** on the answer sheet.

EXAMPLE		ANSWER
Miranda:	Hello Jason. How are you?	
Jason:	0	D

Miranda:	Did you enjoy the pop concert?	**A**	I didn't miss much because there was a large video screen too.
Jason:	16		
Miranda:	Did you have a good seat?	**B**	It was brilliant, thanks. The best one I've ever been to.
Jason:	17		
Miranda:	But could you see everything?	**C**	Yes, it was great because everyone in the concert hall was singing.
Jason:	18		
Miranda:	And did the band play your favourite song?	**D**	I'm very well, thank you.
Jason:	19	**E**	Yes, they played most of them.
Miranda:	I like it when people do that.	**F**	Not bad. I wasn't near the front. But everyone was standing up, so it didn't matter.
Jason:	20		
Miranda:	Oh, it sounds wonderful.	**G**	I think so because there were no empty seats.
		H	So do I. Everyone enjoyed it, so they sang that song again at the end.

Part 4

Questions 21 – 27

Read the article about Debbie Sullivan.
For questions **21 – 27**, mark **A, B** or **C** on your answer sheet.

Storyteller

Debbie Sullivan's a very busy woman. She's got ten children. Every morning she wakes up at six o'clock. The older children get up at six-thirty and start school at eight-thirty. Debbie spends most days at home with her babies, cooking and cleaning. She doesn't have time to go out to work, but she doesn't mind her life. She'd like to have more children. Debbie's husband, Bob, works in an office. He doesn't enjoy it, but he earns lots of money. Debbie spends most of it on food and clothes for the children.

Debbie likes the evening best. After dinner, she sits down in the living-room and tells the children a story before they go to bed. She doesn't read from a book, because these are her own stories. Every week she tells a different story that starts on Monday and ends on Sunday. Once the children are asleep, Debbie can relax. But she doesn't sit and watch television with Bob. She writes her latest story in a notebook before she forgets it.

Bob sent one of Debbie's stories to a competition in a newspaper and it won. They said she should become a writer, but Debbie wasn't sure that she was good enough. But the children thought it was a great idea, so she decided to try. She took them to a zoo. They liked the elephant best, so Debbie wrote a story about it. The book company loved it. You can now buy this story in the shops.

EXAMPLE		**ANSWER**
0 Debbie has		
A six children.	**B** eight children.	**C** ten children. **C**

---

21   Debbie would like to

    A go out more.   **B** get a job.   **C** have another baby.

22   Debbie's husband

    A earns very little money.   **B** doesn't like his job.   **C** goes shopping after work.

23   Debbie tells the children a story

    A at dinner time.   **B** before they go to bed.   **C** to send them to sleep.

24   Every night, Debbie

    A reads from the same book.   **B** starts a new story.   **C** tells part of a story.

25   After telling a story, Debbie

    A tells Bob about it.   **B** tries to remember it.   **C** watches television.

26   Debbie decided to become a writer because

    A her children wanted her to.   **B** her husband asked her to.   **C** she knew she could do it.

27   Debbie wrote a story about the elephant because

    A it's her favourite animal.   **B** her children liked it.   **C** the company told her to.

Part 5

Questions 28 – 35

Read the article about a musical instrument.
Choose the best word **(A, B** or **C)** for each space **(28 – 35)**.

For questions **28 – 35**, mark **A, B** or **C** on the answer sheet.

THE UKELELE

A ukulele .....**0**..... like a guitar. You hold it in .....**28**..... same way and it has four strings which make a sound .....**29**..... you play it. The main difference is that the ukelele is smaller. That is why it makes a different type .....**30**..... sound to a guitar. A lot of people .....**31**..... the ukelele about fifty years ago, including .....**32**.....famous singers and movie stars. .....**33**..... fact, Marilyn Monroe plays one in the famous film called *Some Like it Hot*. But not .....**34**..... people play the ukulele these days. Anne Harris, who plays the ukelele in a pop band, says that this is surprising because it is very easy. Anyone .....**35**..... learn to play their favourite tunes really quickly.

EXAMPLE			ANSWER
0 **A** is	**B** does	**C** has	**A**

28	**A** a	**B** the	**C** very
29	**A** which	**B** when	**C** how
30	**A** of	**B** at	**C** on
31	**A** plays	**B** playing	**C** played
32	**A** some	**B** any	**C** lots
33	**A** In	**B** By	**C** For
34	**A** much	**B** many	**C** few
35	**A** did	**B** need	**C** can

Part 6

Questions 36 – 40

Read the descriptions of things you find in a bathroom.
What is the word for each one?
The first letter is already there. There is one space for each other letter in the word.

For questions **36 – 40**, write the words on your answer sheet.

EXAMPLE	ANSWER
0 You wash your hands with this.	s o a p

36   You stand under running water in this.   s _ _ _ _ _

37   You can see yourself in this.   m _ _ _ _ _

38   You use this to make your hair look nice.   c _ _ _

39   You hold this when you clean your teeth.   t _ _ _ _ _ _ _ _

40   You dry yourself with this.   t _ _ _ _

WHAT IS TESTED

Part 6: Word-completion task (1 mark for each correct answer)
This tests your ability to understand dictionary definitions. A dictionary definition is an explanation of a word: in Paper 1, the words can be nouns, adjectives or verbs.

In Part 6 you:
- read 5 dictionary definitions
- can see the first letter for each word
- can see the number of letters for each word
- must write the word with the correct spelling

The words are all from the same topic. The topic could be *in a restaurant*, *holidays*, *jobs* etc.

ADVICE

Read the instructions and the situation.

EXAMPLE: *Read the descriptions of things you find <u>in a bathroom</u>.*

All the words you write should be things you always find in a bathroom.

soap ✔   radio ✘   shower ✔   mirror ✔   chair ✘   comb ✔   toothpaste ✔   table ✘   towel ✔

Look carefully at the dictionary definition:

- is it asking for a verb, noun or adjective etc?

EXAMPLES:

If you want a room in a hotel, you can phone and **do** this first = verb	(book)
You go **here** to borrow books. = noun/place	(library)
You use **this** to open a bottle of wine. = noun/object	(corkscrew)
You use this **kind of** airplane ticket to go and come back. = adjective	(return)

- is there a preposition that can help you?

You can put your clothes **on** this.	(hanger)
You can put your clothes **in** this.	(wardrobe)

- if the word is a noun, is it plural or singular?

These are sometimes made of cotton and you wear **them** on your feet.	(socks)
Apples and oranges are examples of **this**.	(fruit)

PRACTICE ACTIVITIES

You can do this **after** you do Part 6 on page 44.

Vocabulary task: This helps you organize and record your new vocabulary. It is useful for all parts of KET.

If you want to remember and use new vocabulary well, you could:

- separate vocabulary into different topics
- show the part of speech (noun/verb/adjective/adverb etc)
- show the word stress
- use a dictionary to show you the pronunciation of a word
- show if a noun is countable or uncountable etc.

EXAMPLE:	**In a restaurant**	**Illness**
	a waiter	a cold
	the menu	flu (uncountable noun)
	to order	medicine (uncountable noun)
	spicy (adj)	sore (adj)

- write the preposition if a verb or adjective usually uses one

EXAMPLE

to listen to music   to be interested in something

- write an example sentence so you can see how to use a word

EXAMPLES

to enjoy: *I enjoy going to movies.* (enjoy + ing)
to invite: *Sarah invited me to her party.* (invite + someone)

- write a translation for the word (but be careful – not all the words translate exactly)
- write a synonym (an English word with the same meaning)

EXAMPLES: to book a table = to reserve unhappy (adj) = sad

- write an antonym (an English word with the opposite meaning)

EXAMPLES: a tall man/a short man   hot/cold

- write a collocation

EXAMPLES

to send	an email
to receive	a fax
	a letter

a tall	building/man
a high	mountain/temperature

Exercise 1

Write the words in the box under the 3 topic headings.
Add the part of speech (a/an/uncountable noun/to/adj).
Underline the word stress to words with two or more syllables.
Use a dictionary if you need help.

Write down 2 nouns* for each verb in the box.

~~supermarket~~	~~reserve~~	~~spicy~~	tourist	salt	buy
stir	saucepan	assistant	expensive	hotel	chef
customer	spend	warm	department store	passport	cooker
delicious	sale	fry	foreign	board	beach

Shopping	Holidays	Food
Nouns a supermarket	Nouns	Nouns
Verbs	Verbs to reserve – an airplane ticket* a table*	Verbs
Adjectives	Adjectives	Adjectives spicy

Exercise 2

1   What is the opposite of *expensive*?   c _ _ _ _

2   What does *foreign* often describe?   c _ _ _ _ _ _/l _ _ _ _ _ _ _/f _ _ _

3   What is the opposite of *delicious*?   d _ _ _ _ _ _ _ _ _

4   What word usually goes with *salt*?   p _ _ _ _ _

5   This is a machine that cooks food.   c _ _ _ _ _

6   This is a person that cooks food in a restaurant.   c _ _ _

Part 7

Questions 41 – 50

Complete this letter.
Write ONE word for each space.

For questions **41 – 50**, write the words on your answer sheet.

Dear Paula,

I am having a great time here (**EXAMPLE**: ......at.....) the seaside. The hotel is right next
.....**41**.... the beach. I ......**42**.... already been swimming twice – it was lovely. Tomorrow, we
.....**43**.... going on a coach trip to visit a farm ......**44**.... they grow bananas. ......**45**.... are lots of
banana farms here.

At breakfast this morning I had ......**46**.... glass of banana juice. I have never tried this drink
.....**47**...., but I like it very ......**48**.... I'm going to buy some to bring home ......**49**.... me, then you
can taste ......**50**.... too.

I hope you're not working too hard.

Love

Gary

Part 8

Questions 51 – 55

Read the information about a girl who wants a weekend job.
Complete the information on the application form.
For questions **51 – 55**, write the information on your answer sheet.

---

                                                          18 Tower Rd
                                                          Cardiff
                                                          Wales

Dear Sir/Madam

My name is Sally Wilkes. I was born in Canada and lived
there for 16 years. I am now 17 years old and at the moment
I am at college from Monday to Friday, so can only work
weekends. I used to be a shop assistant at Star Fashions,
Chester Street in Cardiff, but would now like to work in a
coffee bar.

Yours faithfully

Sally Wilkes

PART-TIME JOBS

APPLICATION FORM

Name: *Sally Wilkes*

Address: **51**

Age: **52**

Nationality: **53**

Which days can you work?   **54**

What type of work have you done before? **55**

Part 9

Question 56

Your friend doesn't know anything about your party next week.
Write a note to your friend.
Tell him/her:

- where the party is

- how to travel there

- what to bring

Write **25–35** words.
Write your note on your answer sheet.

Language tasks

You can do these **before or after** you answer question 56 on page 49.

Exercise 1

Read question 56 on page 49. Read the example answer/note below.
How does the note start?
How does the note end?
Does the note include the 3 points in the question?

> Hi Paul
>
> I'm having a barbecue party on Saturday from 3pm in our garden.
> You can take the 51 bus from the station – it stops right outside
> my house. Please bring a few hamburgers.
>
> I hope you can come.
>
> James

Exercise 2

In Part 9, the three points often include *what/where/when/why/how* questions.

Match the questions **1 – 8** with the answers **a – h**. Use the words in bold to help you.

Write a note to your friend.

Say:

1	**when** the party is.	a	It's **on the corner** of the street, **next to** the bank.
2	what the person **looks like**.	b	It's **warm** and **humid**.
3	**why** you have to change the plan.	c	I need it this weekend **because** I have a test on Monday.
4	**where** the restaurant is.	d	I usually **take the subway** and then **walk** for ten minutes.
5	**how you spend** the weekend.	e	It's starting **at 9pm**.
6	what **the weather** is like.	f	She's quite **tall** and she has **long red hair**.
7	**why** you want the book.	g	I can't come **because** I have so much work to do.
8	how you **get to work** every day.	h	I usually **go shopping** with my friends.

Exercise 3

Fill in the gaps to complete each sentence.

Function	Sentence	
1. Making arrangements	L _ _ 's	go to that new restaurant.
	We c _ _ _ _	
2. Saying where and when	We are meeting	o _ _ _ _ _ _ the cinema.
		at my house.
		in f _ _ _ _ of the restaurant.
		_ _ Monday.
		_ _ 3pm.
3. Changing a time/date	_ _ _	we meet on Saturday instead?
	Why _ _ _ '_	
4. Explaining why you can't go somewhere/ meet someone	I can't come b _ _ _ _ _ _ I have a job interview then.	
	I have a job interview then, _ _ I can't come.	
5. Making an invitation	W _ _ _ _ you _ _ _ _ to come to my birthday party on Saturday?	
	I'm cooking dinner for friends on Saturday.	
	W _ _ _ _ you _ _ _ _ to come?	
6. Giving advice	You s _ _ _ _ _	wear warm clothes when you come to Sweden.
	I s _ _ _ _ _ _ you	
7. Making requests	Please _ _ _ _ _ you help me move to my new house next week?	
	_ _ _ _ _ I borrow your car on Wednesday evening?	

Exercise 4

Read the answer to question 56 below. (Don't look at page 50!) Can you remember the right words? Underline the words you think are correct.

Hi Paul

(1) **I have/I'm having** a barbecue party (2) **on/at** Saturday from 3pm (3) **on/in** our garden. You (4) **will/can** take the 51 bus from (5) **a/the** station – it (6) **stops/is stopping** right outside my house. Please bring (7) **a little/ a few** hamburgers.

I (8) **hope/wish** you can come.

Bruce

TEST TWO

PAPER 2: LISTENING (30 minutes)

Part 1

Questions 1 – 5

You will hear five short conversations.
You will hear each conversation twice.
There is one question for each conversation.
For questions **1 – 5**, put a tick (✓) under the right answer.

EXAMPLE

0   How many people were at the party?

20	30	50
A ☐	**B** ✓	**C** ☐

1   What type of soup does Paul choose?

  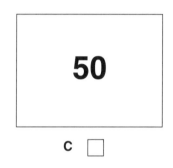

    A ☐   **B** ☐   **C** ☐

2   What time does the play start?

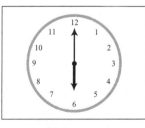 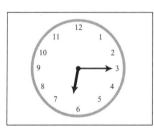 

    A ☐   **B** ☐   **C** ☐

3　What is Ben going to do tonight?

A ☐　　　　　　　　　　B ☐　　　　　　　　　　C ☐

4　How much will the woman pay for the coffee?

A ☐　　　　　　　　　　B ☐　　　　　　　　　　C ☐

5　Which mirror will they buy?

A ☐　　　　　　　　　　B ☐　　　　　　　　　　C ☐

PRACTICE ACTIVITIES

Language tasks: You should do this **after** you do Part 1 on pages 52 and 53.

In Part 1, you sometimes listen to: numbers, prices, dates, times, shapes/sizes and directions.

Numbers

Exercise 1a: How do you pronounce these numbers?

3	13	30
4	14	40
5	15	50
6	16	60

Listen to recording 41 to check your answers.

Exercise 1b: Listen to recording 42. Circle the numbers from Exercise 1a that you hear.

Exercise 1c: How do you pronounce these numbers?

33	303	333
55	505	555

Listen to recording 43 to check your answers.

Prices

Exercise 2: How do you pronounce these prices?

$50	£50	£55	£505	£550
£2.10	£8.15	£10.99	£5.75	£4.30

Listen to recording 44 to check your answers.

Dates

Exercise 3a: How do you pronounce these dates?

1st May   2nd January   3rd October   4th June

Listen to recording 45 to check your answers.

Now write the full word for the dates below.

EXAMPLE: *1st = first 2nd = second 3rd = third 4th = fourth*

5th = ...   6th = ...   7th = ...   8th = ...   9th = ...   10th = ...

11th = ...   12th = ...   13th = ...   14th = ...   15th = ...   16th = ...

20th = ...   21st = ...   22nd = ...   30th = ...

Exercise 3b: Listen to recording 46. Circle the dates that you hear.

Times

Exercise 4: How do you pronounce these times?

10.00am	10.00pm	1.00	1.10	1.15
1.30	1.40	1.45	1.50	1.55

Listen to recording 47 to check your answers.

Shapes + Sizes

Exercise 5: Match the words in the box with a table. Then complete the sentences

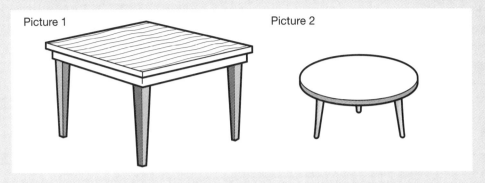

Picture 1   Picture 2

| long | round | big | short | square | small |

Picture 1: a ...., ... table with .... legs

Picture 2: a ...., ... table with .... legs

Directions

Exercise 6: Choose a word in the box to finish each sentence.

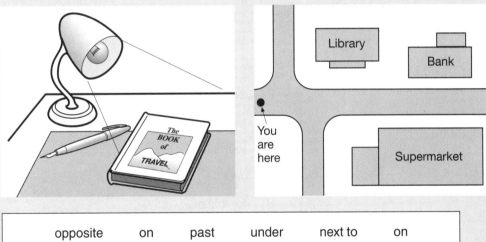

| opposite | on | past | under | next to | on |

Where is the pen?   Where's the bank?

It's .... the table.   It's .... the supermarket.
.... the book.   .... the library.
.... the lamp.   .... the left.

Part 2

Questions 6 – 10

Listen to Fiona talking about the people in her class at school.
What does each person want to be in the future?
For questions **6 – 10**, write a letter **(A – H)** next to each person.
You will hear the conversation twice.

EXAMPLE	ANSWER
0 John	H

Person		**Job**	
6 Suzie	☐	**A** artist	
7 Bob	☐	**B** doctor	
8 Mary	☐	**C** farmer	
9 David	☐	**D** pilot	
10 Anna	☐	**E** teacher	
		F actor	
		G journalist	
		H footballer	

Part 3

Questions 11 – 15

Listen to Rita talking to her friend about a market.

For questions **11 – 15**, tick (✓) **A, B** or **C.**
You will hear the conversation twice.

EXAMPLE	ANSWER
0 When did Rita go to the market?	
A on Monday	☐
B on Wednesday	✓
C on Saturday	☐

11 Where is the market?

A in North Street ☐

B in Hill Street ☐

C in Wood street ☐

12 How did Rita travel?

A by taxi ☐

B by bus ☐

C by bicycle ☐

13 What did Rita buy?

A a book ☐

B a music CD ☐

C a film on video ☐

14 How much did she spend?

A £3.50 ☐

B £4.50 ☐

C £7.50 ☐

15 Who did she meet?

A her cousin ☐

B her neighbour ☐

C her dentist ☐

WHAT IS TESTED

Part 3: Multiple choice (1 mark for each correct answer)

This tests your ability to understand an informal dialogue.
In Part 3, you listen to two people having a conversation either on the telephone or face to face. There are five multiple choice questions. You choose from **A**, **B** or **C** answers/options.

ADVICE

Look at the first line of the instructions. This tells you about the situation: who the speakers are, where the speakers are, or what the speakers are talking about.
The speakers talk about all **3** answers. Only **1** of the answers matches the question.
There are usually **1** or **2** questions that test your ability to understand numbers.
There is sometimes a question that tests your ability to understand days of the week.
The language in the questions may be different to the language the speakers use.
Read the 5 questions and answers **before** you listen to the recording. This will help you **predict** the kind of information or language you hear in the recording.

PRACTICE ACTIVITIES

You can do this **before or after** you do Part 3 on page 57.

Prediction task

Read the five questions from Test 2 Paper 2 Part 3 below.
Circle the words/phrases you think are connected to the 5 questions (1 or 2 answers may be possible).

EXAMPLE: *When did Rita go to the market?*
           a "… I saw it …"   b "… I went there …"   c "… I work there …"   d "… I bought some T-shirts …"
           (Answer = b)

11   Where is the market?
      a   "… in a small road …"   b   "… every Monday and Tuesday …"
      c   "… by bus …"   d   "… quite large …"

12   How did Rita travel?
      a   "… I went by bicycle …"   b   "… It's near my house …"
      c   "… Did you get a bus? …"   d   "… just ten minutes …"

13   What did Rita buy?
      a   "… I spent £25 …"   b   "… My cousin came with me …"
      c   "… I got some new shoes …"   d   "… The market was cheap …"

14   How much did she spend?
      a   "… I got it for £10 …"   b   "… Three things for myself …"
      c   "… The whole afternoon …"   d   "… It cost £15 …"

15   Who did she meet?
      a   "… A friend told me about the market …" b   "… I saw my neighbour …"
      c   "… My sister was at the market too …"   d   "… The bus driver told me where to go …"

Part 4

Questions 16 – 20

You will hear a telephone conversation about a washing machine.
Listen and complete the questions **16 – 20**.
You will hear the information twice.

WASHING MACHINE REPAIRS

Customer's name: Angela White

Problem with machine: **16** .... *not working.*

Time of appointment: **17**

Customer's address: **18** 24 .... *Street*

Customer's phone number: **19**

Name of repair man: **20**

Part 5

Questions 21 – 25

You will hear some information about a coach trip.
Listen and complete the questions **21 – 25**.
You will hear the information twice.

COACH TRIP

To:	Manchester
Day of trip:	**21**
Time the coach leaves:	**22**
Price for students:	**23**
Where to buy your ticket:	**24**
Don't forget to take:	**25**

You now have eight minutes to write your answers on the answer sheet.

TEST TWO

PAPER 3: SPEAKING (8–10 minutes)

Part 1 (5-6 minutes)

Here are some questions you might hear in the Speaking paper.

What's your name?

How do you spell your surname?

What do you do/study?

Do you like it? Why/Why not?

Do you often eat in a restaurant?
        Why/Why not?

What did you eat yesterday?

Tell me about the type of food you like.

If you are in class, work with a partner.

Student A: Ask the questions.

Student B: Listen and answer the questions.

Now change roles.

Student A: Ask the questions.

Student B: Listen and answer the questions.

If you are working alone, you can answer the questions and record yourself.

When you play the cassette, listen and think about what you said:

•   did you know all the vocabulary you needed?

•   did you use the right tenses?

•   do you think your pronunciation of words was clear?

PRACTICE ACTIVITIES

You can do this **before or after** you do Part 1 on page 60.

Language task

Exercise 1

In Part 1, you may need to talk about the <u>past, present and future</u>.
Look at the questions. Which **3** answers are correct/Which **1** is not correct?

1   What do you do?

    a   I'm a student. I go to university in Sao Paulo.
    b   I work for an export company in Beijing.
    c   I am work in a large bank in Paris.
    d   I'm a doctor in a hospital in Geneva but right now, I'm studying English.

2   What did you eat yesterday?

    a   I was eating traditional Korean food. It's called 'kimchi'.
    b   I didn't have breakfast.
    c   I only had a sandwich for lunch.
    d   I ate lots of food – salad, steak, french fries, some cheese.

3   Have you travelled to any other countries?

    a   I've been to Argentina and Chile.
    b   Yes, I have. I went to Korea last year.
    c   I've been to Sweden two years ago.
    d   No, I haven't. It's too expensive!

4   Tell me about your future plans.

    a   I want to go to Australia to visit my friends.
    b   I go to the USA. I have a long holiday there.
    c   If I pass my school exams, I'll go to university.
    d   I'm going to look for a new job.

Exercise 2

Now answer these questions. Write your answers. Write a full sentence.

1   Where do you come from?

2   What do you do?

3   Where do you live?

4   What do you do in your free time?

5   Tell me something about your family.

6   What did you do at the weekend?

7   What did you do last night?

8   What did you eat yesterday?

9   When did you start to learn English?

10   Tell me something about your last holiday.

11   Have you been to any other countries?

12   What are you going to do this weekend?

13   Tell me something about your plans for the future.

If you are in class, work with a partner.
Your partner asks you the questions above – in any order.
You answer. (But don't read your answers. Remember them.)

If you are working alone, read the questions and answer them (but don't read your answers. Remember them). Record yourself and compare your spoken answers to your written answers. Are they the same?

Exercise 3

In Part 1, you may need to talk about your likes and dislikes.
Read the question and the answers **A**, **B** and **C**. Which answers are correct? Which answers are wrong?

Question: Do you like your job?

1	**A** Yes, very much. ✓	**B** No, not much. ✓	**C** Yes, too much. ✗
2	**A** Yes, I do.	**B** Yes, I like.	**C** Yes, I am.
3	**A** No, I don't.	**B** No, I don't like	**C** No, I'm not.
4	**A** Yes, I love it.	**B** Yes, it's great.	**C** It's not bad.
5	**A** It's boring sometimes.	**B** It's bored sometimes.	**C** I'm bored sometimes.
6	**A** I like to meeting customers.	**B** I like meeting customers.	**C** I like meet customers.

Exercise 4

Now answer these questions. Write your answers. Write a full sentence.

1   Do you like your job/your studies?

2   Do you enjoy sport?

3   Do you like watching films?

4   Do you enjoy eating at restaurants?

5   Tell me what you enjoy doing in your free time.

Now say the answers – with a partner, by yourself or use a tape recorder.

In the Speaking paper, you do not need to use a full sentence every time you speak, but it is a good way to show the examiner how much English you know.

Part 2 (A) (3–4 minutes)
Candidate A, here is some information about a play at the theatre.
Candidate B, you don't know anything about the play, so ask **A** some questions about it.
Now **B**, ask **A** your questions about the play and **A**, you answer them.

Candidate A – your answers

Candidate B – your questions

BURTON THEATRE
15 Park Road
This week's play: 'Cats' by A. Webber 7.30pm Monday–Saturday
Seats £15.00, £17.50, £20.00 Students £12.50 (Mondays only)
Theatre Snack Bar: open before and after the play

PLAY AT THE THEATRE
where/theatre?
name/play?
time/play?
student price?
eat/drink?

Part 2 (B)
Now **Candidate B**, it's your turn to have some information.
Candidate B, here is some information about a football match.
Candidate A, you don't know anything about the football match, so ask **B** some questions about it.
Now **A**, ask **B** your questions about the football match and **B**, you answer them.

Candidate B – your answers

Candidate A – your questions

FOOTBALL MATCH
City Stadium
Sat 14th March at 15.00
England vs. Scotland
Tickets:£35, £45, £75 No Parking – please come by bus or train

FOOTBALL MATCH
date/match?
teams?
cheapest ticket?
time/start?
car park?

PRACTICE ACTIVITIES

You can do this **before or after** you do Part 2(B) on page 63.

This exercise will help you ask for help when you don't understand.

Exercise 1

Read the dialogue between Akemi and Nozomi below.

a Which words/phrases show that someone understands?
Underline them.

b Which words/phrases show that someone doesn't understand or needs help?
Draw a wavy line under them.

c Which words/phrases show that someone tries to help or explain something?
Underline them twice

d Which words/phrases does someone use when they need time to think?
Draw two wavy lines under them.

Examiner:	Akemi, here is some information about a football match. Nozomi, you don't know anything about the football match, so ask Akemi some questions about it. Now Nozomi, ask Akemi your questions about the football match and Akemi, you answer them.
Nozomi:	What is the date of the football match?
Akemi:	You mean, when can you see the football match?
Nozomi:	Yes.
Akemi:	Oh, it's on the 14ᵗʰ March. That's a Saturday.
Nozomi:	I see. OK. What teams are there?
Akemi:	Teams? Oh, er, England and Scotland. The English team and the Scottish team.
Nozomi:	Right. England and Scotland. How much is the cheapest price, please?
Akemi:	Price? Do you mean what price are the tickets?
Nozomi:	Yes – the cheapest ticket.
Akemi:	The cheapest ticket is … er, let me see, £35.
Nozomi:	That's not bad. What time does the match start?
Akemi:	It starts at 3 o'clock.
Nozomi:	3 o'clock. Alright. And what about the car park?
Akemi:	Sorry, can you say that again please?
Nozomi:	Yes, I mean, is there a car park near to the football match?
Akemi:	No, there is no parking there. You must come by bus or train.
Nozomi:	Thank you.

More useful language

When you don't understand, you can say (to the examiner or your partner):

> *Sorry, I didn't understand.*
> *Can you say that again, please?*
> *Can you repeat that, please?*

When you don't understand <u>part</u> of the information/sentence, you can say:

EXAMPLE: *"You need to take the train to Liverpool"*   *"Sorry, which train do I need?"*
　　　　　　　"How do you spend your free time?"   *"You mean – what do I do in my free time?"*

Exercise 2

Read the phrases/sentences below. Circle the ones which are correct. There may be one or two correct answers in each line.

a　Sorry, I don't understand./Sorry, I didn't understand./ Sorry, I'm not understand.

b　Can you tell that again?/Can you say that again?/Can you repeat that?

c　What do you mean?/What is your meaning?/What means this?

d　Sorry, I didn't hear you./Sorry, I'm not hearing you./Sorry, I haven't heard you.

e　I didn't catch that./I didn't receive you/I didn't get what you said.

f　Sorry, what the cost of that was?/Sorry, what did you say about the cost?/Sorry, what was the cost of that?

Exercise 3

When you don't understand part of the information/sentence you hear, you can repeat some of the first speaker's sentence and stress the part you didn't understand.

EXAMPLE: "You need to take the train to Liverpool"　"Sorry, _which_ train do I need?"
　　　　　　"How do you spend your free time?"　"You mean - what do I _do_ in my free time?"

Underline the word which must be stressed.

a　"My name is Caroline Haag."

　　"Sorry, what was your name?"

b　"What time does the train depart?"

　　"You mean, what time does the train leave?"

c　"The sports centre closes at 9.30 on weekends."

　　"Sorry, what time does it close?"

d　"Students get a 15% discount."

　　"Sorry, how much is the discount?"

e　"The match is at the City Stadium."

　　"Sorry, where is it?"

f　"What sort of TV programmes do you like?"

　　"You mean, what kind of programme?"

TEST THREE

PAPER 1: READING AND WRITING (1 hour 10 minutes)

Part 1

Questions 1 – 5

Which notice **(A – H)** says this **(1 – 5)?**
For questions **1 – 5**, mark the correct letter **A – H** on your answer sheet.

EXAMPLE	ANSWER
0 You might be late.	**H**

1   You must buy a ticket soon.

2   We will try to see you straight away.

3   You don't have to pay to go here.

4   You will pay less for dinner here this evening.

5   We now close later.

A
> ### BOOKSHOP
> Closing at 2pm – today only

B
> **COLLEGE DINNER**
> *Please show ticket at the gate*

C
> ## HAIRDRESSER'S
> APPOINTMENTS NOT ALWAYS NECESSARY

D
> ### LIBRARY
> NOW OPEN
> FROM 9am TILL 6pm
> (NOT 5pm)

E
> ### Greens Restaurant
> *½-price meals (11am-10pm today)*

F
> **QUEENS THEATRE**
> BOOK NOW
> – ONLY A FEW SEATS LEFT

G
> **Free concert
> in the park**
>
> **Everyone
> welcome!**

H
> DELAYS ON MOST TRAINS EXPECTED TODAY

PRACTICE ACTIVITIES

Language task: This helps you think about the grammar you sometimes see in notices **A – H**.

In different parts of the Reading paper, you need to understand or use <u>present simple passive</u> or <u>past simple passive</u>.

Exercise 1

Read these two dialogues:

Situation: People are waiting at the train station
line 1   **Jane:** "Do you think the train will come on time today?"
line 2   **Sue:** "No, I expect there will be a delay as usual!"

line 3   **John:** "Excuse me, is the train going to be on time today?"
line 4   **Station manager:** Sorry, delays are expected on most trains today."

When Sue speaks:

In Sue's opinion, the train will be late.	(True/False)
In line 2, the subject is 'I'.	(True/False)
In line 2 'expect' is a present simple verb.	(True/False)
'I expect there will be a delay' is an active sentence.	(True/False)

When the station manager speaks:

It is only the station manager who expects the train will be late.	(True/False)
In line 4, the subject is 'delays'.	(True/False)
In line 4, 'are expected' is talking about the present.	(True/False)
'delays are expected on most trains' is a passive sentence.	(True/False)

We use the passive:

• when an action or event is the most important thing

EXAMPLE   "All our oil is imported from other countries."
             The important thing is 'our oil is imported'. The oil doesn't come from our country.
             The person or people who import the oil are not important.

• when we don't know who does/did an action

EXAMPLE   "My car was stolen last week."
             The important thing is now I don't have a car.
             I don't know who stole my car.

• when the speaker/writer doesn't <u>want</u> to say who is responsible for an action

EXAMPLE   "Some coffee was spilt on the computer."
             The speaker doesn't want to say to his boss: 'I spilt the coffee'.
             The speaker just tells his boss about the problem.

How the passive is formed:

Present simple passive		

subject +
 	
Examples:
  All our oil
  Our employees
	is
	are
	
	is
	are
		+ past participle
		
		imported (from other countries)
		given (a bonus once a year)

Past simple passive		

subject +
 	
Examples:
  My car
  The robbers
	was
	were
	
	was
	were
		+ past participle
		
		stolen (last week)
		arrested (yesterday)

Exercise 2

In Part 1, there are sometimes passive forms in the notices and signs.
Because a notice or a sign must be short, they don't use the auxiliary verbs **is + are** in passive forms.

Read the signs and notices below.

Write a full sentence. Use an auxiliary verb and add any other words that you need.

EXAMPLE   Delays on most trains expected today.

Delays on most trains ......*are*......... expected today.

1   *No photography allowed in exhibition.*

No photography .... allowed in .... exhibition.

2   Hotel reception: Door locked at 11.30pm.

Hotel reception: .... door .... locked at 11.30pm.

3   **Lunch served every day 1–2pm.**

Lunch .... served every day .... 1–2pm.

4   *Half-price tickets sold after 6pm.*

Half-price tickets ....

5   Waitress wanted: evenings + weekends

....

Part 2

Questions 6 – 10

Read the sentences about sport.
Choose the best word **(A, B** or **C)** for each space.
For questions **6 – 10**, mark **A, B** or **C** on your answer sheet.

EXAMPLE			ANSWER
0 Amy and Kazu .... playing volleyball.			
A want	**B** enjoy	**C** agree	**B**

6   They both play volleyball very ....
    A   better   **B**   well   **C**   far

7   They decided to .... a volleyball club last month.
    A   join   **B**   add   **C**   go

8   The team .... one evening a week for training.
    A   looks   **B**   sees   **C**   meets

9   Amy and Kazu have already .... lots of friends at the club.
    A   done   **B**   made   **C**   taken

10   They .... to play in a match soon.
    A   feel   **B**   think   **C**   hope

Part 3

Questions 11 – 15

Complete the five conversations.
For questions **11 – 15**, mark **A, B** or **C** on your answer sheet.

EXAMPLE	ANSWER
What do you do?	
A I'm happy.	
B I'm a student.	**B**
C I'm going home.	

11	I'm sorry I'm late.	**A**	That's a problem.
		B	I do too.
		C	It doesn't matter.

12	Will the plane arrive soon?	**A**	It lasts two hours.
		B	In about ten minutes.
		C	An hour ago.

13	That's really kind of you.	**A**	You did too.
		B	Very well thanks.
		C	You're welcome.

14	What does that mean?	**A**	No idea.
		B	No, not much.
		C	I don't think so.

15	I can't lend you any money.	**A**	I'm afraid so.
		B	Sorry about that.
		C	That's alright.

Questions 16 – 20

Complete the conversation between two friends.
What does Mark say to Anna?
For questions **16 – 20**, mark the correct letter **A – H** on your answer sheet.

EXAMPLE		ANSWER
Anna:	Where are you going on holiday this year, Mark?	
Mark:	0	**H**

Anna:	I spent two weeks at the beach last year. It was sunny every day.	**A**	I've got a video about them. Do you want to watch it?
Mark:	16	**B**	No. We stayed in the mountains. It was much cooler.
Anna:	But you've been to Hawaii. Wasn't it really warm there?		
Mark:	17	**C**	I want to go.
Anna:	I see. I don't know where to go this year. Do you think I would like it there?	**D**	I didn't know that. Was that this year?
Mark:	18	**E**	Oh, I don't like hot places very much.
Anna:	That sounds interesting. I'd love to see them.		
Mark:	19	**F**	It's too expensive to go there.
Anna:	OK, thanks. Well, if you like colder places, you could go to Canada. My brother went there.	**G**	Yes, probably. The mountain birds and flowers are beautiful.
Mark:	20	**H**	I don't know yet.
Anna:	Yes, last month. He went there for his job. And he did some ski-ing too.		

WHAT IS TESTED

Part 3: Three-option multiple choice (questions **11 – 15**) Matching (questions **16 – 20**) (1 mark for each correct answer).
This tests your ability to understand conversations/spoken English.

For questions **11 – 15**, you finish a two-line conversation by choosing the correct response **A**, **B** or **C**.
For questions **16 – 20**, you read a longer conversation. You choose **5 sentences** from **8 options**. One of the options is an example.

ADVICE

for questions **11– 15**, ask yourself:

what is the <u>function</u> of the sentence/question?

EXAMPLES

"Can I help you with your suitcase?" = the function is an offer. The speaker is offering to carry the listener's suitcase.
"Do you have the time, please?" = the function is a request. The speaker wants to know what time it is.

If you understand the function, it will help you choose the right answer.

for questions **16 – 20**:

- read the main dialogue first.
- think about the function of each sentence. How does the second speaker need to respond?

EXAMPLES

"Is Saturday alright with you?" = the first speaker wants to arrange a time to do something.
"<u>That's fine</u>. I'll bring my camera." = the second speaker says that Saturday is a good time.
or "I don't like jogging in busy streets." = the first speaker expresses his dislike *"<u>Me neither</u>. It's too dangerous."* = the second speaker shows that he has the same opinion.
notice if there are any questions (the questions have a question mark: ?)

EXAMPLES

"Do you want me to drive you to the airport?"
The answer could be *"No thanks. Sarah is taking me."* or *"Yes, please. That's very kind of you."*
or "<u>Would</u> you like to come for a coffee with us?"
The answer could be *"I'<u>d</u>* (*would) love to. When are you going?"* or *"That <u>would</u> be nice. When?"*
notice if the subject and/or object in one line and the next line are the same.

EXAMPLES

"What time does <u>the train</u> leave?" = *"<u>It</u> goes at 3.05 pm."*
"Have you ever been to <u>Paris</u>?" = *"I went <u>there</u> years ago. <u>It's</u> probably different now."*

PRACTICE ACTIVITIES

You can do this **before or after** you do Part 3 on page 70.

Matching task: This helps you think about the function of the first sentence and what response you need.

Exercise 1

Underline the correct function for each question or statement. The first question is done as an example.

Question/Statement	The speaker is:
1 What do you do?	asking about <u>someone's occupation</u>/plans for the near future
2 What are you doing?	asking about someone's plans for the near future/daily routine
3 How do you feel?	asking about someone's free time/emotions or health
4 I hope to go to university.	saying something is not possible/talking about his plans
5 I've lost my ticket!	talking about a problem: he had in the past/he has now
6 I'm sorry I'm late.	apologizing/explaining
7 Will the plane arrive soon?	asking about: an everyday timetable/the future
8 When did you get here?	asking about: a fact in the past/a possible future
9 How long is the film?	asking about: the length of the film/when the film starts
10 You played very well.	telling someone: You were good in that game of tennis./You are always good at tennis.
11 How are you?	asking about someone's: emotions or health/nationality
12 That's really kind of you.	saying: thank you/you should be kinder
13 What does that mean?	asking about: someone's opinion/the meaning of some information
14 Did you enjoy the film?	saying: Do you want to see a film?/Was the film good?
15 Are you coming with us?	asking about someone's: plans/opinions
16 I can't lend you any money.	asking his friend for money/saying 'no' to his friend.
17 Did he damage the car?	asking about: a past situation/a possible future situation
18 You didn't remember my birthday.	complaining to a friend/inviting a friend

Exercise 2

Match the first speaker's question/statement with the 2nd speaker's response.

	1st speaker		2nd speaker
1	What do you do?	A	I'm happy.
2	What are you doing?	B	I'm a student.
3	How do you feel?	C	I'm going home.
4	I hope to go to university.	A	You need to buy another.
5	I've lost my ticket.	B	I do too.
6	I'm sorry I'm late.	C	It doesn't matter.
7	Will the plane arrive soon?	A	It lasts two hours.
8	When did you get here?	B	In about ten minutes.
9	How long is the film?	C	An hour ago.
10	You played very well.	A	You did too.
11	How are you?	B	Very well thanks.
12	That's really kind of you.	C	You're welcome.
13	What does that mean?	A	No idea.
14	Did you enjoy the film?	B	I don't think so.
15	Are you coming with us?	C	No, not much.
16	I can't lend you any money.	A	I'm afraid so.
17	Did he damage the car?	B	Sorry about that.
18	You didn't remember my birthday.	C	That's alright.

Do the next exercise **after** you do questions 16–20 on page 71.

Exercise 3

This helps you think about the language in the longer dialogue. It helps you think about the type of words and phrases you need to look for.

Read the dialogue. The first question is done as an example.

Anna: Where are you going on holiday this year, Mark?

Mark: I don't know **(1)** yet.

Anna: I spent two weeks at the beach last year. It was sunny **(2)** every day.

Mark: Oh, I don't like hot places **(3)** very much.

Anna: But **(4)** you've been to Hawaii. Wasn't it really warm there?

Mark: No. **(5)** We stayed in the mountains. It was much cooler.

Anna: I see. I don't know where to go this year. Do you think I would like it there? **(6)**

Mark: Yes **(7)**, probably. The mountain birds and flowers are beautiful.

Anna: That sounds interesting. I'd love to see them. **(8)**

Mark: I've got a video about them. Do you want to watch it?

Anna: OK, thanks. **(9)** Well, if you like colder places, you could go to Canada.
           My brother went there. **(10)**

Mark: I didn't know that. **(11)** Was that this year? **(12)**

Anna: Yes, **(13)** last month. He went there **(14)** for his job. And he did some ski-ing too.

1   What doesn't Mark know? = *where he is going on holiday*
2   Find two more adjectives that are similar to 'sunny'.
3   What 'place' does Anna mention next?
4   When Anna says '<u>But</u> you've been to Hawaii' is she showing **a** understanding **b** surprise ?
5   What does Mark mean when he says 'No'?
6   Where is 'there'?
7   What does Mark mean when he says 'Yes'?
8   What does 'them' mean?
9   Why does Anna thank Mark?
10   Where is 'there'?
11   What does 'that' mean?
12   What does 'Was that this year?' mean?
13   What does 'Yes, last month' mean?
14   Where is 'there'?

Part 4

Questions 21 – 27

Read the article about a man who opened a restaurant, and then answer the questions.
For questions **21 – 27**, mark **A, B** or **C** on your answer sheet.

OPENING A RESTAURANT

Twelve months ago Robin Parker left his job at an insurance company. He now runs a restaurant which is doing very well since it opened four months ago.

Opening a restaurant was a big change for Robin. He loves travelling and all his favourite television programmes are about cooking. One day, he read in a newspaper about a doctor who left her job and moved to Italy to start a restaurant. He thought, 'I can do that!' His wife wasn't very happy about the idea, and neither was his father. But his brother, a bank manager, gave him lots of good ideas.

Robin lived in Oxford and had a job in London. He thought both places would be difficult to open a restaurant in, so he chose Manchester because he knew the city from his years at university. He found an empty building in a beautiful old street. It was old and needed a lot of repairs, but all the other buildings were expensive and he didn't have much money.

Robin loves his new work. It's difficult being the boss, but he has found an excellent chef. He says he enjoys talking to customers and some of them have become his good friends. He gets up at 6am and often goes to bed after midnight. It's a long day but he only starts to feel really tired when he takes time off at the weekends.

Robin's restaurant is doing so well that he could take a long holiday. But he's busy with his new idea to open a supermarket selling food from around the world. He's already found a building near his restaurant.

EXAMPLE		ANSWER
0 Robin's restaurant opened		
A four months ago.	**B** eight months ago.	**C** twelve months ago. **A**

21   Robin decided to open a restaurant after he
    A   visited Italy.   **B**   saw a TV programme.   **C**   read a newspaper story.

22   Who helped Robin open his restaurant?
    A   his wife   **B**   his brother   **C**   his father

23   Where is Robin's restaurant?
    A   in Oxford   **B**   in London   **C**   in Manchester

24   Robin chose the building his restaurant is in because
    A   it was old.   **B**   it was cheap.   **C**   it was beautiful.

25   Robin likes
    A   meeting his customers.   **B**   being a good boss.   **C**   trying the chef's dishes.

26   Robin feels most tired
    A   in the mornings.   **B**   at weekends.   **C**   in the evenings.

27   Next, Robin wants to
    A   take a long holiday.   **B**   open a second restaurant. **C**   start another business.

Part 5

Questions 28 – 35

Read the article about the Amazon River.
Choose the best word (**A**, **B** or **C**) for each space.
For questions **28 – 35**, mark **A**, **B** or **C** on your answer sheet.

THE AMAZON RIVER

The Amazon ....**0**.... the second longest river in the world today. It carries more water than ....**28**.... other river. The Amazon starts ....**29**.... the centre of Peru and travels across Brazil ....**30**.... about four thousand kilometres. ....**31**.... the river gets to the end of its long journey, it opens into the Atlantic Ocean. At ....**32**.... point, it is eighty kilometres wide. Brazil, with a third of the world's rainforest, has fifty-five thousand kinds of flowering plant. Half of these are ....**33**.... found in the Brazilian Amazon. ....**34**.... is possible that many of these plants could become important medicines. This is perhaps why many people today ....**35**.... to help protect this special area of the world.

EXAMPLE			ANSWER
0 **A** is	**B** was	**C** be	**A**

28	**A** all	**B** each	**C** any
29	**A** in	**B** on	**C** to
30	**A** during	**B** up	**C** for
31	**A** What	**B** When	**C** How
32	**A** this	**B** a	**C** their
33	**A** nearly	**B** only	**C** once
34	**A** There	**B** One	**C** It
35	**A** want	**B** wants	**C** wanting

Part 6

Questions 36 – 40

Read the descriptions of things you might need on holiday.
What is the word for each one?
The first letter is already there. There is one space for each other letter in the word.

For questions **36 – 40**, write the words on your answer sheet.

EXAMPLE		ANSWER
0	You need to buy this before you travel by plane.	ticket

36	When you arrive in another country, you have to show this.	p _ _ _ _ _ _ _
37	You pack your clothes in this.	s _ _ _ _ _ _ _
38	This place has a reception where you can get the key to your bedroom.	h _ _ _ _
39	You'll need this to take photos with.	c _ _ _ _ _
40	If you go camping, you will stay in this.	t _ _ _

Part 7

Questions 41 – 50

Complete this postcard.
Write ONE word for each space.

For questions **41 – 50**, write the words on your answer sheet.

Dear Josh,

Happy New Year! We (**EXAMPLE** ....are..) spending New Year in the mountains. We arrived two days ....**41**.... . My grandmother has ....**42**.... lovely house here. We are going to stay with ...**43**.... for one week. ....**44**.... snowed yesterday, but today is sunny ....**45**.... warm. Yesterday we climbed up ....**46**.... the top of a mountain. It ....**47**.... us three hours to get there. I love it here in winter more ....**48**.... in summer. Tonight ....**49**.... is going to be a big party in the centre ....**50**.... the village.

See you soon,

Maria

WHAT IS TESTED

Part 7: Open cloze (1 mark for each correct answer)
This tests your ability to complete a short note or letter with the correct grammar or vocabulary.

In Part 7, you
- read a short note or letter (or a short note and the reply)
- fill 10 gaps with one word
- must spell the words correctly

ADVICE

- read all of the note or letter so you understand the general meaning/situation
- read the whole sentence when you decide what word to write
- look at the words before and after each gap

PRACTICE ACTIVITIES

You can do this **before or after** you do Part 7 on page 77.

Language task
This helps you think about what 'clues' to look for in the text.
Exercise 1
Read the sentences from the letter and answer the questions below.

Dear Josh,

We ....**0**.... *spending New Year in the mountains.*

1   'spend*ing*' is part of a continuous verb form. We also use an auxiliary verb to make a continuous form. What auxiliary do we need? (Remember: this is a postcard and the writer is talking about her holiday now)

   *We arriv**ed** two days* ...**41**... .

2   What tense is 'arrived'?   What time word do we often use with this tense?

   My grandmother has ...**42**... *lovely house here.*

3   'House' is a countable noun.   What do we often write in front of a countable singular noun?

   We are going to stay with ...**43**... *for one week.*

4   What kind of word usually comes after 'to stay with ....'? In the sentence before, who is the subject?

   ...**44**... *snowed yesterday, but today is sunny* ...**45**... *warm.*

5   'Snowed' is a past simple verb. We need a subject before a verb. What subject/one word do we use for the weather?

6   When 2 adjectives have different meanings we can use *but* to join them.
   EXAMPLE: *The day was cold **but** sunny* or *The meal was expensive **but** not very tasty*. What word do we use to join two adjectives that have a similar meaning?

   Yesterday we climbed ...**46**... *the top of a mountain.*

7   The verb *climb* needs a preposition. What is it? (We often use the same preposition with the verbs *go, travel, walk* and *send* – when someone or something moves from one place to another place)

   It ...**47**... *us three hours to get there.*

8   You need to use a verb. Which verb do we use to talk about 'how long' an action is? (in this sentence, the action is three hours) What time (past/present/future) is the sentence talking about?

   I love it here in winter more ...**48**... *in summer.*

9   We often use *more* when we compare two things. What word/conjunction usually comes after *more* in a comparing sentence?

*Tonight ...**49**... is going to be a big party in the centre ...**50**... the village.*

10   What word do we often use to introduce a new idea/subject which is followed by the verb *to be*?

11   What word comes after *in the centre* .... *in the middle*........ *at the top* .... etc?

Exercise 2

Pronouns

Choose the correct pronoun in each sentence.

1   **Maria:**   "Can I borrow <u>you/your/yours</u> dictionary, Hari?"
    Hari: "Sorry, I left <u>me/my/mine</u> at home. Why don't you ask Elena if you can borrow <u>she/her/hers</u>?"

2   **Natalia:**   "<u>It's/There's</u> a concert in the park tomorrow."
    Sergei: "I know, but <u>it's/there's</u> so cold now!"
    Natalia: "But <u>it/there</u> is free!"
    Sergei: "Free? <u>It/There</u> will be long queues as well!"

Write the correct pronoun in each gap.

someone	anything	no-one	something	everyone	everything

3   **Michiko:** Who is coming to your party?
    Aya: .... I know!
    Michiko: Shall I bring .... to drink?
    Aya: No, I don't need .... I already bought .... we need.
    Michiko: Can I bring .... with me? She's a friend of mine.
    Aya: OK, but I must give you some directions. .... knows where the party is yet!

Verb forms

Read the dialogues. Choose the correct verb form. Use the words in *italics* to help you.

1   **a**   *How often* <u>do you play/are you playing</u> tennis?
    b   *Usually,* <u>I play/I'm playing</u> *twice a week.*

2   Where do you live?
    Well, *at the moment* <u>I live/I'm living</u> with my parents, but I want to find my own apartment soon.

3   **a**   <u>I am going/went</u> to Tokyo *last week*, on a business trip.
    b   Really? Where <u>are you staying/did you stay</u>?

4   **a**   <u>Are you phoning/Have you phoned</u> Mr Kitano *yet*?
    b   Yes, I <u>spoke/have spoken</u> to him 10 minutes *ago*.
    c   He <u>comes/is coming</u> to London *next week*.

5   Did you see the accident?"
    Yes. I <u>waited/was waiting</u> for the bus *when the truck crashed* into the shop.

6   Do you have any *plans* for the weekend?
    Yes, <u>I visit/I'm going to visit</u> some friends.

7   You look tired.   Yes. I *think* <u>I go/I'll</u> go to bed early *tonight*.

8   What's the problem?
    I can't use my new microwave. *The instructions* <u>are writing/are written</u> in German.

Modals

Choose the correct modal verb(s) for each sentence.

shall	need to	may	have to	need	should
could	must	would	should	can	could

1   ..../................../..................you please send me some information about your courses? (a request)
2   Thank you for the invitation. What time ..../..................I arrive at your house? (asking for a suggestion).
3   San Francisco is wonderful! We ....go to Los Angeles as well, but we aren't sure yet. (possibility)
4   If you don't like your job, you ..../..................look for a new one. (advice)
5   I can't meet you today. My boss said I ..../................../..................finish my report today. (obligation)
6   If you..................somewhere to stay, you are welcome to stay with us.

Connectives

Join the sentences together.

I passed my driving test	**and**	I don't have any money to buy a car!
	but	my English exam!
	because	I had a lot of driving lessons.

You could come to the café with us	**when**	you could go with Jane.
	or	have a coffee there.
	and	you finish work.

Please visit me and my family	**if**	my mother really wants to meet you!
	because	you come to Seoul.
	but	don't come in May.

I'm planning to go to New Zealand	**when**	my cousins live.
	where	Australia next year.
	or	I graduate this year.

Articles

We use 'a'
• to introduce an idea/object/noun for the first time
We use 'the'
• when we talk about an object/noun for the second time/again etc.
• when the speaker/writer believes the listener/reader knows which object/noun he is talking about
• with superlative forms (example: the biggest/the most expensive)
• with times of day (example: in the morning/in the afternoon etc.)
• with positions + locations (example: in the centre/in the east of)

Write an article (a/the) in each gap.

Dear Ella

This is just (1) .... quick note to tell you that I cannot go to (2) .... cinema on Saturday afternoon. I have to meet my brother at (3) .... airport. I haven't seen him for (4) .... long time! I'm taking him to (5) .... local restaurant in (6) .... evening. They make (7) .... best pizza! Would you like to come with us?

Love Jo

Dear Jo

Thanks for (8) .... note. I remember your brother – he's (9) .... youngest in the family, isn't he? I'd love to come to (10) .... restaurant. Is it (11) .... one which is at (12) .... end of your road? Please give me (13) .... call and tell me what time you are going.

Love Ella

Part 8

Questions 51 – 55

Read the information about a student who wants to do a computer course.
Fill in the information on the application form.
For questions **51 – 55**, write the information on your answer sheet.

My name's Jason Perry and I'm from Australia. I'm 19 years old and a student at City College. I read your advertisement in Today Magazine and would like to do one of your computer courses. I have lessons from Monday to Thursday, so I'm only free on Friday. I'm looking for a beginners course. Please send information to me at 22 Kings Road.

COMPUTER TRAINING COURSES

APPLICATION FORM

Name:	Jason Perry
Address:	**51**
Age:	**52**
Nationality:	**53**
Which day(s) do you want to do a course?	**54**
Where did you see our advert?	**55**

Part 9

Question 56

Read this email from your English friend, Jamie.

I hope you are enjoying your holiday. What is the weather like? Where are you staying? Tell me how you are spending your time.

Jamie

Write Jamie an email. Answer the questions.
Write **25–35** words.
Write the email on your answer sheet.

Language tasks: You can do these **before or after** you answer the question on page 81.

Exercise 1
Read question 56 on page 81. Read the example answer/note below.
How does the email start?
How does the email end?
Does the email include the 3 points in the question?

Dear Jamie,
Thanks for your email. I'm having a great time. Every day I go swimming in the morning and diving in the afternoon. It is hot and sunny and we are staying in a lovely hotel near the beach.
Love Paula

Exercise 2
When you write your answer to Part 9, you <u>must</u>
write the name of the person you are writing to: **EXAMPLE** *Dear Jamie*
write your name at the end: **EXAMPLE** *Love (your name)*

Beginning a note/an email
Look at some ways to begin a note/email below. Decide which:
4 are good ways to begin.
1 is wrong.
1 is for a business letter (**not** a good way to begin your answer in KET)

Dear Peter Jones,	To Peter,	Dear Peter,
Dear friend	Hi Peter,	Peter,

Ending a note/an email
Look at some ways to end a note/email below. Decide which:
1 is for a business letter (**not** a good way to begin your answer in KET)
1 is at the end of an invitation
1 is at the end of a letter making an arrangement

See you soon Claudia	Love Claudia	Claudia
Yours from Claudia	I hope you can come! Claudia	Yours sincerely Claudia

You can also end a note/email by writing:
Claudia   - for informal/neutral notes/emails/letters
Yours, Claudia   - for more friendly notes/emails/letters
Love Claudia   - for notes/emails/letters to good friends or family

Exercise 3
Vocabulary: Use a dictionary to help you.

Describing the weather
a   Write the adjectives:

It is	warm / h _ _ / b _ _ _ _ _ _	here.
It has been	c _ _ _ _ _ /cold / f _ _ _ _ _ _ _	in (place).
	dry (opposite =) w _ _	
	sunny (opposite =) c _ _ _ _ _	

b   Write the verbs: It is s _ _ _ _ _ _ _/r _ _ _ _ _ _ _ .   The sun is s _ _ _ _ _ _ .
c   Write the noun: There was a big s _ _ _ _ yesterday. (strong wind/rain)

Places to stay

Fill in the grid: tick the correct boxes.

	in the city	at the beach	in the country -side	in the mountains	near the motorway	someone can cook all your meals for you	this can be quite cheap	the family who own this often live and work here	you might share a room with people you don't know
four star hotel	✓	✓	✓	✓		✓			
motel									
ski-lodge									
campsite									
backpacker's hostel									
pension									
bed and breakfast									

Things to do on holiday
Choose the correct verb for each noun/noun phrase.

try   go x 7   buy x 2   write   visit   take   play x 2

1 .... sightseeing   **2** .... a souvenir   **3** .... tennis

4 .... walking in the mountains/forest   **5** ..../............................ postcards
around the town/city

6 .... shopping   **7** .... museums   **8** .... sailing

9 .... new food   **10** .... diving   **11** .... photographs

12 .... swimming   **13** .... volleyball   **14** .... horse-riding

TEST THREE

PAPER 2: LISTENING (30 minutes)

Part 1

Questions 1 – 5

You will hear five short conversations.
You will hear each conversation twice.
There is one question for each conversation.
For questions **1 – 5**, put a tick (✓) under the right answer.

EXAMPLE

0   How many people were at the party?

      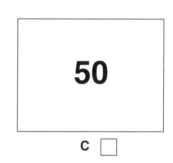

A ☐   B ✓   C ☐

1   What does the woman want to drink?

A ☐   B ☐   C ☐

2   Which woman is the new maths teacher?

A ☐   B ☐   C ☐

3   What did the boy see at the zoo?

A ☐

B ☐

C ☐

4   How does the man travel to work?

A ☐

B ☐

C ☐

5   What is the date of the concert?

A ☐

B ☐

C ☐

Part 2

Questions 6 – 10

Listen to Maria telling Tom about her house.
Which colour did she paint each room?
For questions **6 – 10**, write a letter **(A–H)** next to each room.
You will hear the conversation twice.

EXAMPLE	ANSWER
0 Hall	**B**

Person

6   living room   ☐

7   dining room   ☐

8   kitchen   ☐

9   bedroom   ☐

10   bathroom   ☐

Job

A   brown

B   pink

C   white

D   yellow

E   blue

F   green

G   purple

H   orange

Part 3

Questions 11 – 15

Listen to Sonia asking about a game.

For questions **11 – 15**, tick (✓) **A, B** or **C**.
You will hear the conversation twice.

EXAMPLE	ANSWER
0 The game is called	
A Go.	☐
B Start.	✓
C Sorry.	☐

11 The shop started selling the game

    A this week.   ☐

    B last week.   ☐

    C two weeks ago.   ☐

12 To play the game, you must have

    A one player only.   ☐

    B two players or more.   ☐

    C four players or more.   ☐

13 To play the game, you should be

    A five years old or younger.   ☐

    B eight years old or older.   ☐

    C sixteen years old or older.   ☐

14 One game normally takes

    A one hour.   ☐

    B less than one hour.   ☐

    C more than one hour.   ☐

15 If you buy the game, you could win

    A a holiday.   ☐

    B some money.   ☐

    C another game.   ☐

Part 4

Questions 16 – 20

You will hear a telephone conversation about booking a taxi.
Listen and complete the questions **16 – 20**.
You will hear the information twice.

ABC TAXI COMPANY

Name of customer:	*Harry Todd*
Wants to go to:	**16**
Time and day:	**17** *Saturday*
Customer's address:	**18** *39 .... Road*
Phone number:	**19**
Name of driver:	**20**

Part 5

Questions 21 – 25

You will hear some information about a boat trip.
Listen and complete questions **21 – 25**.
You will hear the information twice.

BOAT TRIP

Day of trip:	**21**
Meet at:	10am
Meeting place:	**22** the .... (on River Street)
Price for students:	**23** £
On the boat, you can buy:	**24**
Boat will stop at:	**25** in Hamble Village

You now have eight minutes to write your answers on the answer sheet.

WHAT IS TESTED

Part 4: Gap-fill (1 mark for each correct answer)

This tests your ability to understand and write information in a gap-fill exercise.

In Part 4, you listen to two people having a conversation on the telephone or face to face. There are 5 questions: you have to write down 5 pieces of information. You write words or numbers.

ADVICE

Look at the first line of the instructions. This tells you about the situation: who the speakers are, where the speakers are, or what the speakers are talking about.

You sometimes need to write: names of people or addresses/street names.

When the name is difficult or unusual, one of the speakers dictates the name for you. When the speaker dictates a name, you must spell it correctly.

You often need to write: numbers, times, dates and prices.

PRACTICE ACTIVITIES

You should do this **before or after** you do Part 4 on page 88.

Pronunciation and listening task

Exercise 1: What are the sounds of the alphabet in English?
Say each letter. Listen to recording 48 and check your answers.

A   B   C   D   E   F   G   H   I   J   K   L   M
N   O   P   Q   R   S   T   U   V   W   X   Y   Z

Exercise 2: Listen to recording 49. Write the surnames of the people below.

a   Peter ....

b   Simon ....

c   Jane ....

d   Julie ....

e   Andrew ....

f   Emily ....

g   Steven ....

Exercise 3: Listen to recording 50. Complete the addresses below.

a   12 .... Road

b   44 .... Avenue

c   6 .... Street

d   81 .... Avenue

e   16 .... Street

f   158 .... Road

TEST THREE

PAPER 3: SPEAKING (8–10 minutes)

Part 1 (5–6 minutes)

Answer these questions.

What's your name?

How do you spell your surname?

Do you work or are you a student?

What do you do/study?

Do you like it? Why/Why not?

Where did you go on your last holiday?

Did you enjoy it? Why/Why not?

What other country would you like to visit? Why?

If you are in class, work with a partner.

Student A: Ask the questions.

Student B: Listen and answer the questions.

Now change roles:

Student B: Ask the questions.

Student A: Listen and answer the questions.

If you are working alone, you can answer the questions and record yourself.

When you play the cassette, listen and think about what you said:

*   did you know all the vocabulary you needed?

*   did you use the right tenses?

*   do you think your pronunciation of words was clear?

PRACTICE ACTIVITIES

You can do this **before or after** you do Part 1 on page 90.

This exercise will help you explain something when you don't know the English word/words.

Read the conversation between an examiner and Eric below.
<u>Underline</u> **3** examples of: when Eric explains something
  when he doesn't know the English word - or
  when he wants to be sure the examiner understands him.

Examiner:	What's your name?
Eric:	Eric Cherix
Examiner:	How do you spell your surname?
Eric:	It's C-h-e-r-i-x
Examiner:	Do you work or are you a student?
Eric:	Now I'm a student.
Examiner:	What do you study?
Eric:	I study, er, hotel management. I have to think about, er, who works at the hotel, the advertising, the money that the hotel needs.
Examiner:	Do you like it?
Eric:	Yes, it's very interesting. It's difficult, but I like it.
Examiner:	Where did you go on your last holiday?
Eric:	I went to the Seychelles with some friends.
Examiner:	Did you enjoy it?
Eric:	Yes and no. The hotel was nice and the sea was very warm, but it was very, er, too quiet. I mean, there were not many things to do there.
Examiner:	What other country would you like to visit?
Eric:	I'd like to go to Brazil.
Examiner:	Why?
Eric:	Because I want to see the …er, I don't know how you say it, but the Brazilian people have a special party – everyone dances, everyone wears something special.
Examiner:	OK, thank you.

Three ways to explain what you mean

When you are not sure about the English word/words for something, you can

- say *"I don't know how you say it, but…"* and explain with a longer sentence (example 3 above)

- say the same thing in a different way (example 2)

- give an example (example 1)

Part 2 (A) (3–4 minutes)

Candidate A, here is some information about tennis lessons.

Candidate B, you don't know anything about the tennis lessons, so ask **A** some questions about them.
Now **B**, ask **A** your questions about the tennis lessons and **A**, you answer them.

Candidate A – your answers   **Candidate B** – your questions

TENNIS LESSONS	TENNIS LESSONS
12 lessons (Mondays 6–8pm)	where?
at Green Park, Beachside Road	many lessons?
for ages 10–16	for everybody?
only £75!	expensive?
Please bring sports shoes!	need / bring?

Part 2 (B)

Now **Candidate B**, it's your turn to have some information.

Candidate B, here is some information about a language school.
Candidate A, you don't know anything about the language school,
so ask **B** some questions about it.
Now **A**, ask **B** your questions about the language school and **B**, you answer them.

Candidate B – your answers   **Candidate A** – your questions

SWAN LANGUAGE SCHOOL	LANGUAGE SCHOOL
10 Station Road, Bridgetown	name/school?
Daytime & evening lessons – 6 days per week	all languages?
	when/lessons?
Courses in English, German, Spanish & French	good/teachers?
Excellent teachers!	address?

PRACTICE ACTIVITIES

You can do this **before or after** you do Part 2 on page 92.

Read the dialogue between Joy and Takeshi below.
There are **7** grammar mistakes. Find the mistakes and correct them.

Joy:	Takeshi, what is name of the language school?
Takeshi:	It called the Swan Language School.
Joy:	Can I studying all languages here?
Takeshi:	No, there is only courses in English, German, Spanish & French.
Joy:	When the lessons are?
Takeshi:	The lessons are in the daytime and in the evening, six days a week.
Joy:	Does the school have good teacher?
Takeshi:	Yes, the teachers are excellent.
Joy:	And how is the address of the school?
Takeshi:	It's 10 Station Road, Bridgetown.
Joy:	Thank you.

....

....

....

....

....

....

....

....

....

....

....

TEST FOUR

PAPER 1: READING AND WRITING (1 hour 10 minutes)

Part 1

Questions 1 – 5

Which notice **(A – H)** says this **(1 – 5)**?
For questions **1 – 5**, mark the correct letter **A – H** on your answer sheet.

EXAMPLE	ANSWER
0　You cannot leave your car here.	**C**

1　You should go to the other entrance.

2　You cannot eat your lunch here.

3　Don't leave anything here when you get off.

4　You should go outside to use your telephone.

5　There may be a lot of traffic here.

A

> **PAYPHONE** - 20 metres on right
> *(opposite Kay's Café)*

B

> **VISIT OUR COFFEE SHOP**
> **BEFORE YOU LEAVE**

C

> **CAR PARK CLOSED**

D

> **NO FOOD OR DRINK**
> **IN THE**
> **MUSEUM**

E

> **SWITCH OFF MOBILE PHONES**
> **WHEN ENTERING HOSPITAL**

F

> **WET PAINT!**
> *PLEASE USE BACK DOOR*

G

> **SLOW! ACCIDENT ON MOTORWAY**

H

> **PASSENGERS LEAVING THE TRAIN:**
> **PLEASE REMEMBER YOUR LUGGAGE**

Part 2

Questions 6 – 10

Read the sentences about music lessons.
Choose the best word (**A, B** or **C**) for each space.
For questions **6 – 10**, mark **A, B** or **C** on your answer sheet.

EXAMPLE			ANSWER
0 I'm .... to play the guitar.			
A teaching	**B** knowing	**C** learning	**C**

6   I've .... ten music lessons altogether.
     A booked   **B** asked   **C** paid

7   I .... to the first lesson yesterday.
     A arrived   **B** visited   **C** went

8   My brother .... me his old guitar.
     A took   **B** gave   **C** bought

9   The lesson was more .... than I thought it would be.
     A hard   **B** difficult   **C** heavy

10   I'm going to .... at home for one hour every day.
     A practise   **B** take   **C** follow

Part 3

Questions 11 – 15

Complete the five conversations.
For questions **11 – 15**, mark **A , B** or **C** on your answer sheet.

EXAMPLE	ANSWER
What do you do? **A** I'm happy. **B** I'm a student. **C** I'm going home.	**B**

11   Did you enjoy the film?   **A** It's too nice.
                                    B Not really.
                                    C Thanks for asking.

12   Nice to see you again.   **A** I don't remember.
                                   B You too.
                                   C Don't mention it.

13   Hurry up or we'll be late.   **A** It's not early.
                                        B There's no time.
                                        C Let's go now then.

14   Dinner is ready.   **A** Oh good!
                         B I'll cook tonight.
                         C Not yet.

15   I've lost my wallet.   **A** Not again!
                             B I'm afraid so.
                             C It doesn't matter.

Questions 16 – 20

Complete the conversation between two friends.
What does Sam say to Harry?

For questions **16 – 20**, mark the correct letter **A – H** on your answer sheet.

EXAMPLE		ANSWER
Harry:	Hello Sam. Nice to see you!	
Sam:	0	**A**

Harry:	Fine thanks. I started a new job this week.	**A**	You too! How are you?
Sam:	**16**	**B**	I haven't bought anything in that shop for ages.
Harry:	I'm working at the clothes shop in Weldon Road.	**C**	Yes, you're right. It's very interesting.
Sam:	**17**		
Harry:	I think so. They're still training me at the moment.	**D**	How long does that last?
Sam:	**18**	**E**	I don't know what that is.
Harry:	Only a week. Then I'll be ready to work in the shop, helping customers.	**F**	What are you doing?
Sam:	**19**	**G**	Thanks for telling me. I will do.
Harry:	Well, you should come in and see me one day soon. There's a sale on next week.	**H**	Oh yes, I know which place you mean. Do you like it there?
Sam:	**20**		
Harry:	Anyway, I've got to go now. My lunch break has nearly finished.		

Part 4

Questions 21 – 27

Read the article about an actor.
Are sentences **21 – 27** 'Right' **(A)** or 'Wrong' **(B)**?
If there is not enough information to answer 'Right' **(A)** or 'Wrong' **(B)**, choose 'Doesn't say' **(C)**.
For questions **21 – 27**, mark **A, B** or **C** on your answer sheet.

JUAN FERNANDEZ

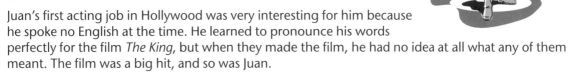

As a child in Spain, Juan Fernandez wanted to be a footballer. That was before he broke his foot at the age of fifteen. After this, he decided to become an actor. He went to acting school, which he enjoyed more than his old school. But after only a year there, he was offered work at the National Theatre and he left the school without getting his diploma.

At the theatre he met film-maker Antonio Garcia who invited him to act in a film called *Camarero*. Antonio's film was watched in many other countries, and soon film-makers in Hollywood wanted to meet the good-looking young actor.

Juan's first acting job in Hollywood was very interesting for him because he spoke no English at the time. He learned to pronounce his words perfectly for the film *The King*, but when they made the film, he had no idea at all what any of them meant. The film was a big hit, and so was Juan.

He then decided to learn some English. Because he was never good at languages as a child, he went back to school. Since then Juan has made nine films in English which have all been big hits.

Although Juan is very busy, he enjoys his career in Hollywood and has a big house there, which he loves. But he would like to return to the musical theatre in Europe now and again to practise what he learnt at acting school. He would like to show people that he's still a good singer!

EXAMPLE			**ANSWER**
0 When he was a young child, Juan wanted to be an actor.			
A Right	**B** Wrong	**C** Doesn't say	**B**

21 Juan left acting school before the end of the course.
    A Right   **B** Wrong   **C** Doesn't say

22 Juan met Antonio Garcia when they worked on a play together.
    A Right   **B** Wrong   **C** Doesn't say

23 The film *Camarero* helped Juan to get to Hollywood.
    A Right   **B** Wrong   **C** Doesn't say

24 In *The King*, Juan only understood some of the words he was saying.
    A Right   **B** Wrong   **C** Doesn't say

25 Juan taught himself to speak English.
    A Right   **B** Wrong   **C** Doesn't say

26 Juan likes working in Hollywood.
    A Right   **B** Wrong   **C** Doesn't say

27 Juan prefers working in the theatre to making films.
    A Right   **B** Wrong   **C** Doesn't say

WHAT IS TESTED

Part 4: Reading a text with seven questions (1 mark for each correct answer)

This tests your ability to understand **the main ideas** in a magazine or newspaper text.

In Part 4, you answer **7** questions by
either   choosing from **A**, **B** or **C**
or   choosing **Right**, **Wrong**, **Doesn't Say**

ADVICE

Read the text first so you can understand the general meaning.
Don't worry if you can't understand every word. You can find the answer in a group of words, one sentence or maybe two sentences.
Read the questions carefully and <u>underline</u> the most important parts.

EXAMPLES

When he was a young <u>child</u>, Juan wanted to be an <u>actor</u>.
Juan <u>left acting school</u> before the end of the course.
The questions follow the order of the text.

Multiple-choice A B C

Read the question carefully. All **3** answers may be in the text but only **1** answer is the right one.

EXAMPLE

Nora loved to draw and paint when she was at school and she wanted to become an artist. Her parents both worked for a bank and when Nora left school at 18, her mother suggested she got a job at the same one. Nora had an interview, but decided she wanted to travel around the world for a year.

Nora's mother wanted Nora to
A become an artist.   *No. <u>Nora</u> wanted to be an artist.*
B work in a bank.   *Yes. In the same bank as her parents.*
C travel to different countries.   *No. <u>Nora</u> wanted to travel.*

Right/Wrong/Doesn't Say:

'Wrong' means the question says something **different** to the text.
EXAMPLE   *Text:*   Mr Green rarely ate meat, except on Sundays.
          Question: Mr Green never ate meat. = WRONG

'Doesn't Say' means the question asks for information that is **not in** the text.

EXAMPLE   *Text:*   Mr Green rarely ate meat, except on Sundays.
          Question: Mr Green ate beef on Sundays. = DOESN'T SAY

PRACTICE ACTIVITIES

You can do this **before or after** you do Part 4 on page 97.

Comprehension task: This helps you think about the meaning of the questions and the information in the text.

Read questions **0 – 27** from the text. Answer the other questions below them.

1   *0   When he was a young child, Juan wanted to be an actor.*
The question says 'young child'. In the text, how old is Juan when he decides to become an actor?

....

....

2   *21   Juan left acting school before the end of the course.*
The question says '<u>before</u> the end of the course'. The text says 'But after <u>only</u> a year.' What does 'only' suggest in this situation? Which other four words later in the paragraph also suggest that Juan does not finish his course?

....

....

3   *22   Juan met Antonio Garcia when they worked on a play together.*
We know that Juan is an actor at the National Theatre. We know that Antonio is a film-maker. Does the text tell us that Antonio was working at the National Theatre too?

....

....

4   *23   The film Camarero helped Juan to get to Hollywood.*
Is it true that only Spanish people saw the film Camarero? Who wanted to meet Juan because they had seen Camarero?

....

....

5   *24   In The King, Juan only understood some of the words he was saying.*
Did Juan speak English in *The King*? Which phrase tells us that he didn't understand the words he was saying in the film?

....

....

6   *25   Juan taught himself to speak English.*
In the text, who decided that Juan needed to learn English? When he was a child, was it easy or difficult for Juan to learn languages? Which five words in the fourth paragraph show us that Juan did not teach himself?

....

....

7   *26   Juan likes working in Hollywood.*
Which noun in the fifth paragraph means 'your job/your work'? Which verb is similar to 'likes'?

....

....

8   *27   Juan prefers working in theatre to making films.*
When we talk about what we prefer, we can use words/phrases like *It's better than* .... or *I like* .... *more than* .... or *I prefer* etc. Are there any words/phrases in the fifth paragraph that show what Juan prefers?

....

....

Part 5

Questions 28 – 35

Read the article about the writer, Beatrix Potter.
Choose the best word (**A, B** or **C**) for each space.

For questions **28 – 35**, mark **A, B** or **C** on your answer sheet.

BEATRIX POTTER (1866 – 1943)

Beatrix Potter was born .....**0**..... London. When she was young, she spent her holidays in the area of England .....**28**.... *The Lake District*. Her family stayed at Wray Castle next to *Windermere*, ...**29**.... of the lakes. Later they had several houses .....**30**.... great gardens. Beatrix loved life in *The Lakes* .....**31**.... always drew pictures of the animals she saw. She was also very good .....**32**.... writing stories. A friend told her .....**33**.... she should make the stories into books. Her first book *The Tale of Peter Rabbit* went on sale in 1901. With the money she earned from .....**34**.... book, she bought a farmhouse in *The Lake District*. She got married when she was forty-seven years old. After that, she spent .....**35**.... time working as a sheep farmer than writing books.

EXAMPLE			ANSWER
0 **A** of	**B** in	**C** from	**B**

28	**A** called	**B** calls	**C** call
29	**A** any	**B** one	**C** some
30	**A** with	**B** to	**C** across
31	**A** so	**B** then	**C** and
32	**A** by	**B** on	**C** at
33	**A** that	**B** which	**C** what
34	**A** these	**B** them	**C** this
35	**A** much	**B** more	**C** most

Part 6

Questions 36 – 40

Read the descriptions of some jobs.
What is the word for each one?
The first letter is already there. There is one space for each other letter in the word.
For questions **36 – 40**, write the words on your answer sheet.

EXAMPLE	ANSWER
0 I work in a hospital, helping the doctors.	n u r s e

36   I fly a plane.   p _ _ _ _

37   People visit me if they have a problem with   d _ _ _ _ _ _
their teeth.

38   I write for newspapers and magazines.   j _ _ _ _ _ _ _ _

39   I drive people to where they want to go.   t _ _ _ d _ _ _ _ _

40   I paint pictures and sell them in shops.   a _ _ _ _ _

Part 7

Questions 41 – 50

Complete these letters.
Write ONE word for each space.

For questions **41 – 50**, write the words on your answer sheet.

Dear Mrs Robinson,

I am **0**(EXAMPLE ....sorry....) I wasn't in your lesson yesterday. I fell off my bicycle ....**41**.... the morning so I could ....**42**.... get to school. The doctor told ....**43**.... that I must stay ....**44**.... home today. Luckily, I ....**45**.... not broken anything. I'm sure I ....**46**.... be back tomorrow. What was yesterday's homework?

Yours,

Karl

Dear Karl,

What ....**47**.... pity about your accident. How ....**48**.... you fall off your bicycle? ....**49**.... wasn't any homework yesterday because we ....**50**.... to York on a school trip.

Best wishes,

J Robinson

Part 8

Questions 51 – 55

Read the information about a talk at a club.
Complete Rachel's notes.
For questions **51 – 55**, write the information on your answer sheet.

Camera Club Meeting
      13/10, 7pm

Room E203

Mike Green (Apex Cameras)

will speak about Photographing Animals

Club Secretary: Tim Harris

Rachel,
Mike phoned. He's going to arrive late. He'll be
here at 7.30pm. He needs a map – can you post
one to him? Also, please put a DVD player in the
room – he wants to show a film. If he's
interesting, we could invite him again to talk
about photographing sport.
Thanks
Tim

RACHEL'S NOTES

Date of meeting:	13th October
Name of visitor:	**51**
He will arrive at:	**52**
Subject of his talk:	**53**
He wants to use our:	**54**
Please send him:	**55**

Part 9

Question 56

Your friend sent you a present for your birthday last week.
Write a note to your friend.

Say:

what you thought of the present

which other presents you had

how you spent your birthday.

Write **25 – 35** words.
Write the note on your answer sheet.

WHAT IS TESTED

Part 8: Information transfer (1 mark for each correct answer)
This tests your ability to understand and find important information in a text.

In Part 8:
* you read 1 or 2 short texts (an email, a note, a letter, an advert, a poster, travel information etc.)
* you use the information to complete a form or some notes
* there are five gaps in the form or notes
* you write one word or a short phrase
* you must spell everything correctly
* you must use capital letters correctly

ADVICE

Read the texts and the form/notes carefully because:
* there are often **2 names** or **2 dates** or **2 occupations** etc in the texts. You must choose and write the correct name/date/occupation etc.
* the information in the texts is not in the same order as the questions in the form/notes.
* you must copy names and addresses etc correctly. Do not make spelling or punctuation mistakes!

PRACTICE ACTIVITIES

You can do this **before or after** you do Part 8 on page 102.

Comprehension task: This helps you think about the information you need to find in the texts.

Read questions **51 – 55** and the texts on page 102. Answer questions **1 – 5** below.

Name of visitor: **51** ....

1 You can see 3 names in the texts: Mike Green, Tim Harris and Rachel.
   Who belongs to the Camera Club?
   Who is just a visitor?

He will arrive at: **52** ....

2 What words in the text mean the same as 'He will arrive at .... ' ?

Subject of his talk: **53** ....

3 Find a synonym for 'talk' ....What is the subject of the talk <u>this time</u>?
   When you write the subject, do you need to use capital letters?

He wants to use our: **54** ....

4 What kind of word comes after 'use our ....' ?

Please send him: **55** ....

5 Which word in the text means the same as 'send'?

Language tasks

Exercise 1: Complete the information below.

Country	Nationality Language
Someone from France	is French / speaks French
Someone from Germany	is .... / speaks ....
Someone from Italy	is .... / speaks ....
Someone from	is Greek / speaks Greek
Someone from Australia	is .... / speaks ....
Someone from	is Polish / speaks Polish
Someone from Japan	is .... / speaks ....
Someone from the USA	is .... / speaks ....
Someone from Brazil	is .... / speaks ....

Exercise 2: Match the occupation in the box to the description below.

manager   police officer   dentist   journalist   teacher   sales assistant   doctor   banker

a This person works in a school.

b This person writes for a newspaper.

c This person looks after your teeth.

d This person might say 'Can I help you?' in a shop.

e You might talk to this person when you need money.

f You visit this person when you are ill.

g This person tells other people what they have to do.

h This person wears a uniform and sometimes has a gun.

Exercise 3: Write a time, a day, a date, a month or a period of time in each gap.

a The class starts at ....
     on ....
     in ....

b The flight leaves at ....
     from ....
     takes ....

Exercise 4: Read the letter. Which words need capital letters? Make the necessary changes.

43 cranwell rd
muswell hill
london

the manager   2 february 2005
the queen elizabeth hotel
1 high street
oxford

dear mr fisher

I stayed at your hotel from monday 25th january to wednesday 27th. Unfortunately, I left a valuable book in my room. It is called history of the americas and it is written in spanish.

Please send it to me and I will pay for the postage.

Yours sincerely

dr anna atkins

TEST FOUR

PAPER 2: LISTENING (30 minutes)

Part 1

Questions 1 – 5

You will hear five short conversations.
You will hear each conversation twice.
There is one question for each conversation.
For questions **1 – 5**, put a tick (✓) under the right answer.

EXAMPLE

0   How many people were at the party?

20	30	50
A ☐	B ✓	C ☐

1   How much will the man pay for the jacket?

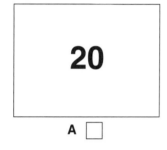   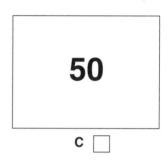

A ☐	B ☐	C ☐

2   Where did the woman have lunch?

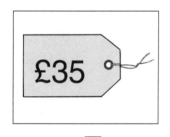   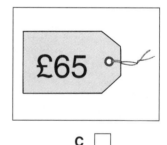

A ☐	B ☐	C ☐

3   What is the girl's favourite subject at school?

Science	History	Geography
A ☐	B ☐	C ☐

4   How will the man travel to London?

A ☐   **B** ☐   **C** ☐

5   Which shop will they go to next?

A ☐   **B** ☐   **C** ☐

Part 2

Questions 6 – 10

Listen to Helena talking about food that people have brought to a party.
Which person brought each thing to the party?
For questions **6 – 10**, write a letter **(A – H)** next to each person.
You will hear the conversation twice.

EXAMPLE	ANSWER
0 Jack	**E**

People

  6   Suzie   ☐

  7   Julie   ☐

  8   Mark   ☐

  9   Tim   ☐

10   Sally   ☐

Food

A   fruit

B   cake

C   sandwiches

D   biscuits

E   drinks

F   pizza

G   sweets

H   salad

Part 3

Questions 11 – 15

Listen to Martin asking about a holiday job.

For questions **11 – 15**, tick (✓) **A, B** or **C.**
You will hear the conversation twice.

EXAMPLE	ANSWER
0 The job is for	
A four weeks.	☐
B six weeks.	✓
C eight weeks.	☐

11   The job is at a

A   café.   ☐

B   hotel.   ☐

C   supermarket.   ☐

12   Each week, the assistant will work

A   twelve hours.   ☐

B   fifteen hours.   ☐

C   twenty hours.   ☐

13   The hourly pay is

A   £5.00.   ☐

B   £5.50.   ☐

C   £5.75.   ☐

14   The assistant will receive

A   free meals.   ☐

B   a taxi to go home.   ☐

C   time off at the weekend.   ☐

15   Martin will meet the manager on

A   Monday.   ☐

B   Thursday.   ☐

C   Saturday.   ☐

Part 4

Questions 16 – 20

You will hear a conversation at a hotel.
Listen and complete the questions **16 – 20.**
You will hear the information twice.

HOTEL BOOKING FORM

First name: David

Surname: **16**

Room type (twin/single/double):   **17**

Cost of room (including discount): **18** £

Meals: **19**

Car number: **20**

Part 5

Questions 21 – 25

You will hear some information about a museum.
Listen and complete questions **21 – 25.**
You will hear the information twice.

WEXFORD HISTORY MUSEUM

Museum opened in: *1923*

Museum shows the history of: **21**

Next museum tour starts at: **22**

Price for tour (per person):   **23** £

Museum shop sells: •   **24**

                              •   books

                              •   **25**

You now have eight minutes to write your answers on the answer sheet.

WHAT IS TESTED

Part 5: Gap-fill (1 mark for each correct answer)

This tests your ability to understand and write information in a gap-fill exercise.

In Part 5, you listen to **1 person** speaking; for example, a tour guide, a college tutor or a friend who leaves a message on the answer phone. There are **5 questions**: you have to write down **5 pieces** of information. You write words or numbers.

ADVICE

Look at the first line of the instructions. This tells you about the situation: what the speaker is talking about. Sometimes you need to write: names of people or addresses/street names.
When the name is difficult or unusual, one of the speakers dictates the name for you. When the speaker dictates a name, you must spell it correctly.

You sometimes need to write: numbers, times, dates and prices. There are exercises in the *Further Practice and Guidance* section in Test 2 Paper 2 Part 1 that can help you.

The speakers usually repeat a word that is difficult.
Part 5 is different to Part 4 because:
In Part 5, you only hear 1 person speak
In Part 5, you need to understand and write more *vocabulary*
In Part 4, there are <u>more</u> numbers, prices, times, dates etc

EXAMPLE

Questions	Answers
Meeting place:	*the park*
Name of book:	*Paris Guide*
Bring:	*warm coat*

PRACTICE ACTIVITIES

You can do this **before or after** you do Part 5 on page 109.

This exercise will help you recognize words in the Listening paper and pronounce words correctly.

Pronunciation and listening task
Exercise 1: <u>Underline</u> the word in each group that has these sounds.

/g/   flight   single   daughter   luggage

/p/   stamp   cupboard   psychiatrist   receipt

/d/   grandmother   sandwich   Wednesday   midnight

Listen to recording 51 and check your answers.

Exercise 2: All of these words have a letter which is not pronounced. <u>Underline</u> the letter.

c|a|s|t|l|e   i|s|l|a|n|d   a|u|t|u|m|n   c|l|i|m|b   l|i|s|t|e|n   s|a|l|m|o|n   l|a|m|b

Listen to recording 52 and check your answers.

TEST FOUR

PAPER 3: SPEAKING (8–10 minutes)

Part 1 (5–6 minutes)
Answer these questions.

What's your name?

How do you spell your first name?

Where do you live?

Do you like living in ....? Why/Why not?

Tell me about your house/flat.

What do you enjoy doing in the evening?

Do you like any sports?

What are you going to do next weekend?

Part 2 (A) (3–4 minutes)

Candidate A, here is some information about a shopping centre.
Candidate B, you don't know anything about the shopping centre,
so ask **A** some questions about it.
Now **B**, ask **A** your questions about the shopping centre and **A**, you answer them.

Candidate A – your answers

Candidate B – your questions

BLUE SKY
shopping centre

more than 50 shops
– for clothes, shoes,
music & books

open every day – 9am–8pm

near city centre   parking for 400 cars

SHOPPING CENTRE

name?

in city centre?

car park?

what / buy?

open Sunday?

Part 2 (B)

Now **Candidate B**, it's your turn to have some information.

Candidate B, here is some information about a camping holiday.
Candidate A, you don't know anything about the camping holiday. Ask **B** some questions about it.
Now **A**, ask **B** your questions about the camping holiday and **B**, you answer them.

Candidate B – your answers   **Candidate A** – your questions

CAMPING IN SCOTLAND

camp-site near mountains & river

2 weeks (August 1st–15th)

Campsite shop sells food and drink

£175 per person

more information: Nevis Holidays (phone 5543026)

CAMPING HOLIDAY

how long?

where?

cost?

shop?

more information?

PRACTICE ACTIVITIES

You can do this **before or after** you do Part 2(B) above.

Read the dialogue between Eva and Anna below.
How well do they do in the Speaking paper?
Does Anna give full answers?
Does Eva respond in a natural way?
Do they explain things well?

Eva:	How long is the holiday?
Anna:	2 weeks. August 1st to August 15th.
Eva:	Yes. Where is it?
Anna:	The campsite is near mountains and river.
Eva:	How much does it cost?
Anna:	£175 per person
Eva:	Is there a shop nearby?
Anna:	What?
Eva:	Is there a shop nearby?
Anna:	What? Oh, er, campsite shop.. there is food and drink.
Eva:	Yes. How do I get more information?
Anna:	Nevis Holidays has more information. 5543026.
Eva:	I finished.

Key and Explanation,
Listening Scripts
and
Sample Answer Sheets

KEY AND EXPLANATION

TEST ONE
Reading and Writing page 4

Part 1
1 C   2 E   3 G   4 A   5 H

Further Practice and Guidance page 5

Question 1: The question is about 'not driving fast' so the words could be:

car: *car* and *drive* are often in the same sentence or subject of conversation.

slow: *slow* is the opposite of *fast*. *He is a slow driver* is similar to *He is not a fast driver*.

dangerous: It is not a good idea to drive fast when a road is dangerous.

The word that probably isn't in the answer is:

easy: when someone says *You shouldn't drive fast here* – they are giving you a warning or saying that something is a bad idea. When someone says *It is easy to drive* – they are encouraging you.

Question 2: The question says that it is *not possible* or it is *forbidden*, to take pictures. The words could be:

allow: *You are not allowed to do something* can mean the same as *You cannot do something*.

photography: *take a photograph* means the same as *take a picture*.

camera: you need a camera to take a picture.

The word that probably isn't in the answer is:

painting: *painting* has no connection to *photography*.

Question 3: The question warns you, or says it is a bad idea to leave your car somewhere. The words could be:

vehicle: a car is a kind of vehicle

drivers: a driver has to leave his car somewhere when he isn't driving it.

parking: *to leave your car somewhere* can mean the same as *to park your car*.

The word that probably isn't in the answer is:

fast: the question is about where you should park your car, not about how fast you should drive it.

Question 4: The question says that it is not possible to use a credit card. The words could be:

pay: you can pay for something by using money, a credit card, a cheque etc.

buy: you can buy something by using money, a credit card, a cheque etc.

cash: *cash* is another word for *paper money*. If it is not possible to use a credit card, you probably need to use cash.

The word that probably isn't in the answer is:

free: the question is about how you can pay. It isn't about not paying.

Question 5: The question is about *paying less than usual* for something. The words could be:

cheaper: when you *pay less* for something, it is *cheaper*.

sale: when a shop has a *sale*, the things in the shop are cheaper than usual.

price: when you *pay less* for something, the price will be cheaper.

The word that probably isn't in the answer is:

refund: when you don't like something you bought and take it back to the shop, the shop assistant may give you a refund (give you all your money back).

Part 2
6 C   7 A   8 B   9 A   10 B

Part 3
11 C   12 B   13 B   14 A   15 B
16 E   17 C   18 A   19 G   20 H

Part 4
21 B   22 B   23 A   24 C   25 B   26 A   27 B

Part 5
28 B   29 B   30 A   31 B   32 A   33 C   34 A
35 C

Further Practice and Guidance page 10

Exercise 1

1 **Fiona and Murray's baby <u>was</u> born yesterday afternoon.**
We use *was born* because we know exactly when the baby came (yesterday afternoon).

2 **Mum? I'm just calling to tell you the baby <u>has</u> just been born!**
We can use *has been born* to say the baby just came a few minutes ago. But – it's more usual to say, for example, *Maria <u>has</u> just <u>had</u> the baby!*

3 **In the world, a baby <u>is</u> born every three seconds.**
We use *is born* to talk about a fact in the general present.

4 **He's leaving his job <u>in</u> October.**
We use *in* with months.

5 **The concert is <u>on</u> October 25th.**
We use *on* with exact dates.

6 **The party starts <u>at</u> midnight.**
We use *at* with *midnight/midday*.

7 **Simon and Anna will be late. <u>They</u> are coming by bus.**
We use *they* to talk about people.

8 **I'm going to be late. <u>There</u> is a big traffic jam on the motorway.**
We use *there* to introduce a new subject/noun/pronoun.

9 **I don't like these jeans. <u>Those</u> ones look better.**
We use *those* to talk about a plural subject. When the person is speaking, he is probably holding *these jeans* and pointing to *those jeans*.

10 **I've <u>always</u> lived in Paris.**
We can use *always* to connect the past to the present. We often use *always* with present perfect simple tense.

11 Eric still lives with his parents.
We can use *still* to connect the past to the present.

We can use *still* with present simple + present continuous: *Eric still lives* (or – *is still living*) *with his parents*. In this sentence, the speaker is probably surprised that Eric lives with his parents. He thinks Eric should live somewhere else because he is too old to live with them.

We can use *still* with present perfect negative: *The bus still hasn't arrived.*

The speaker thinks the bus is late – it should have arrived before now.

12 Have you found somewhere to live yet?
We can use *yet* for present perfect simple questions and negatives. In this sentence, the speaker knows the other person started (in the past) looking for a new place to live. The speaker wants to know if the other person found a new place between that past time and now.

13 Takeshi didn't know what he wanted to do when he left school.
We can use *when* to talk about a point of time or a period of time. In this sentence, *when* means *after*.

14 He really loved animals so he studied to become a vet.
We can use *so* to talk about the result of something. In this sentence, we understand that *Takeshi loved animals*. The result is: *he studied to become a vet*.

15 He got a job in London which he really enjoys.
We use *which* to talk about the object before. In this sentence, the object is *a job*. You can also write *He got a job in London. He really enjoys his job* but in English, a longer sentence is better than 2 short sentences.

16 Mario went on holiday to France where he met a woman called Claudia.
We use *where* to talk about the place before. In this sentence, the place is *France*.

17 He fell in love with Claudia who was very beautiful.
We use *who* to talk about the person before. In this sentence, the person is *Claudia*.

18 Now he's learning French which he thinks is very difficult.
We use *which* to talk about the object before. (see the answer to question 15). In this sentence, the object is *French*.

19 I'll only go to Germany if I get a good job.
We can use *if* to show what may be possible in the future. The speaker is saying that the only way he will go to Germany is by getting a good job. He isn't sure that he will get a good job. It is just a possibility.

20 I'm going to Germany next week because I have a new job in Berlin.
We use *because* to talk about the *reason* for something. Why is the speaker going to Germany? Because he has a new job.

21 Helena, can you send this report to the office in Germany? I've already sent it.
We use *already* to show that something happened in the past/ before now. The exact past time is not important. We often use *already* with present perfect.

22 Now I'm a student, I don't have much money.
We use *much* with uncountable nouns. We use *much* in questions and negative forms.

23 We're having some problems with our new software.
We use *some* before plural nouns or uncountable nouns. We use *some* in positive forms . We can also use *some* to make a request : *Can I have some tea, please? Can I have some more time to finish this report?*

24 We could either go ski-ing or sailing.
We often use *either* when we are offering a choice of two things.

25 We don't have any food in the house!
We can use *any* in negative sentences – before countable or uncountable nouns:
He doesn't speak any English. There aren't any good cafes in my town.

26 Excuse me, is anyone using this seat?
We use *this* to talk about one object or subject. In this sentence, the speaker is probably pointing to a seat. Another example: *I don't like this coffee.* The speaker is probably drinking a cup of coffee.

27 The new seat I bought for my office is good for my back.
We can use *the* to introduce a subject/object – when we give some more information to describe the subject/object. In this sentence, the information is *I bought for my office*. Also - it is probably not the first time the speaker talks about the seat.
Another example: *The new restaurant next to the bank is opening tomorrow. Next to the bank* tells us which restaurant the speaker is talking about. The speaker and listener have probably both seen the new restaurant before but the speaker is telling the listener when the new restaurant will open.

Exercise 2

1 *b* the free time I had wasn't enough for me
2 *b* We have some problems. We need to fix them.
3 *b* Just two or three actors are as good as Robert De Niro
4 *a* So you need to learn Spanish before you come here.
5 February, March etc
6 spring, autumn
7 in the evening, in the night
8 Wednesday, Thursday etc
9 any date
10 Easter, Ramadan, etc
11 midday, 3.15 etc
12 much/*a lot of*
13 many
14 many/ a lot of
15 much/a lot
16 many/a lot of
17 much
18 a lot. We can use *quite* with *a lot* but not *many* and *much*.
19 We can use *for* + plural form.
20 *For* shows us the start time to the finish time.
21 We use *during* + a period of time.
22 We can use *during* + plural form.
23 *During* shows us some of the time.
24 We use *since* + a point of time.
25 We can't use *since* + plural form (usually!).

26 *Since* connects the past to the present.
27 We use *since* with present perfect.

28 taller
29 tallest
30 spicier
31 spiciest
32 more expensive
33 most expensive
34 better (than)   (the) best
35 worse (than)   (the) worst

Part 6
36 waiter
37 menu
38 bill
39 kitchen
40 knife

Part 7
41 for
42 to
43 I
44 to
45 who
46 can/could
47 it
48 your/the
49 Is
50 or

Part 8
51 16 West Road, Cambridge
52 Brazilian Disco Music
53 £4.99
54 12 March
55 credit card

Further Practice and Guidance page 16

Exercise 1
Writing about the 3 things:
(1) How big is your house?
(2) What is your room like?
(3) What is the best thing about your house?

Both answer A and B are good. Points 1, 2 and 3 are in a different order but the meaning is still clear and the answers are organized well.

> Dear Chris
> (1) I live in a small apartement with my family.
> (2) I am share a room with my brother so it's a bit untidy.
> (3) I love that our apartement has a nice balcony where I sit in the sun.
> Mario

> Dear Chris
> (3) The best thing of my house is the view – everywhere there are mountain.
> (1) It's quite large so if you come in Japan, you can stay with us.
> (2) My room is full of university books! I have to study hard!
> Love Michiko

Exercise 2
A   spelling mistake = apart~~e~~ment
     grammar mistake = I ~~am~~ share a room

B   2 preposition mistakes = best thing *about* … come *to* Japan
     a mistake with a plural form = there are *mountains*

Exercise 3
a   What do you look like? = appearance
     What are you like?   = personality
     What do you like?   = interests
b   1   What does your friend look like?
         She has   dark hair and she   is   quite tall.
     2   What is your friend like?
         She is   friendly and she   is   really funny.
     3   What does your friend like?
         She likes   playing tennis/to play tennis at weekends.

Exercise 4
1   small
2   younger
3   retired
4   intelligent
5   tall
6   dark
7   quiet
8   new
9   different

TEST ONE

Listening page 18
1 B   2 A   3 B   4 C   5 B

Further Practice and Guidance page 20

Question 1
1   The girl first wanted to have an appointment at 9.30am.
2   'they' probably means 'the dentist' or 'the person who answered the telephone'. In English, we sometimes use 'they' to talk about one person when the person represents a company or when the gender of the person is unimportant.
3   The dentist offered the girl an appointment at 10.00am or at 10.30pm.
4   The girl doesn't want a 10.30 appointment because her class starts at this time.
5   'It should be OK' means
     c   I will have enough time to travel from the dentist's to my class.

Question 2
1   'it' means 'Wellstown'
2   'on the way' means 'between here and Wellstown'
3   'one' means 'a petrol station'
4   'another' means 'a different petrol station'.
5   2 km away = the nearest petrol station
     4km away = the next petrol station after that
     10km away = Wellstown – the place that the woman is driving to

Question 3
What did Monica do at the weekend?
1   Why does the boy ask this question?
     a Before the weekend, Monica told him she planned to go cycling.
2   What does 'in the end' tell us in this sentence?
     b   Monica changed her plans.
3   'that' means 'my friend's new sports car'.

4 'that' means 'going out in the sports car with your friend'.
5 'it' means 'my friend's new sports car'.
6 'the one' means 'the sports car' (in the TV advertisement).

Question 4
1 'Sorry' means **b** No, I haven't got any bananas
2 **b** No
3 'oranges will be fine' means **a** I want to buy oranges
4 The woman wants a kilo of <u>oranges</u>
5 The woman doesn't buy any apples because **b** she has apples at home

Question 5
(1) + (4) = b/future plans
(2)   = a/present time: routines and habits
(3)   = c/past time - when we know exactly when something happened
(5) + (6) = d/past time – to talk about someone's experience + when the exact time is not important

Part 2
6 G   7 H   8 C   9 E   10 F

Further Practice and Guidance page 23

…and the other things were presents from my family too. My <u>brother</u> gave me that <u>red sofa</u>. It was in his <u>flat</u> with <u>two red chairs</u>, but it was too <u>big</u>. He's still got the <u>chairs</u>.

Tina: And what about the <u>table</u> that the <u>CD player's</u> on?

David: My <u>sister</u> gave me that. She bought a <u>new table</u> and chairs when she got <u>married</u>. This is her <u>old</u> one.

Tina: And this <u>desk</u> looks <u>really old</u>.

David: Yeah, it was my <u>grandfather's desk</u> when he was a <u>student</u>. <u>He</u> gave me <u>that</u> and my <u>grandmother</u> gave me that <u>mirror</u> over <u>there</u> on the <u>wall</u> next to the <u>lamp</u>.

Tina: And <u>what</u> about your <u>mother</u>?

David: <u>She</u> bought me those <u>bookshelves</u>. My <u>brother</u> helped me put them on the <u>wall</u>. We put the <u>mirror</u> up at the same time.

Tina: It <u>all</u> looks <u>really nice</u>.

Part 3
11 B   12 C   13 A   14 A   15 B

Part 4
16 LAKE
17 Russian
18 12th January
19 Tuesday
20 £3.50

Part 5
21 eggs
22 2.25
23 tomato
24 television
25 (tele)phone number

TEST ONE
Speaking page 26

Further Practice and Guidance page 27
Part 1
Conversation 1 is 'very good' because the candidate:
• gives quite long answers
• doesn't make many mistakes (I go usually shopping/some informations programmes)
• only hesitates a little bit (It's a bit, er, expensive/ I prefer, er, serious programmes)

This candidate can probably take a higher test than KET.

Conversation 2 is 'not good' because the candidate:
• only gives very short or one-word answers
• makes a lot of <u>basic</u> grammar mistakes (I like there/ I playing guitar/Listen music./Yes, I watch)
• gives the wrong answer to the last question

This candidate makes mistakes, but the most important thing is that **he needs to say more**.

Conversation 3 is 'good' because the candidate
• sometimes gives long answers
• tries hard to communicate his ideas
• makes mistakes, but the message is still clear (It has villages in Switzerland/you make ski-ing/on the countryside)
• finds ways to explain when he doesn't know the word
  (I don't know the English word, er, you make ski-ing not in the mountains – you make it on the countryside.)
• can correct his mistakes quickly (There are many peoples, I mean, people,/so it's bored, er, boring.)
• asks the examiner when he doesn't understand (Sorry – can you repeat that, please?)

This candidate has a good level for KET.

Further Practice and Guidance page 31
Part 2
Exercise 1
The questions in the dialogue are correct, but there are other ways to ask the same questions. Look at Exercise 3 to look at the other ways.

Exercise 2
Roberto: It's called the London Hotel.
Sylvia: <u>OK, The London Hotel</u>, and how many rooms does it have?
Roberto: More than 50 rooms – it's quite large.
Sylvia: <u>Really?</u> and can I have a private bathroom?
Roberto: Er … yes, each room has its own bathroom. You can have a private bathroom.
Sylvia: <u>Great</u>. What about dinner? Can I have dinner in this hotel?
Roberto: Yes, it has an excellent restaurant. You can eat here.
Sylvia: <u>Good</u>. How much does a room cost?
Roberto: It costs $100 for a single room and $150 for a double room.
Sylvia: <u>I see. Thank you</u>.
Roberto: OK, Sylvia, what's the name of the sports centre?
Sylvia: It's, er, the City Sports Centre.
Roberto: OK. <u>Can I play tennis in this sports centre?</u>

Sylvia:	Yes, you can. And also you can go swimming and horse-riding.
Roberto:	<u>That's good</u>. When can I play tennis?
Sylvia:	Everyday, if you want.
Roberto:	<u>Right</u>, and can I eat and drink something at the sports centre?
Sylvia:	Yes, there is a coffee bar with snacks. You can get something here.
Roberto:	<u>That's great</u>, and, er, I'm a student. Is there a cheaper price for a student, for this sports club?
Sylvia:	Yes, the cost is £50 per year but for you, for students, it's £35 a year, OK?
Roberto:	<u>OK</u>. <u>Very good.</u>

Exercise 3: (Mistakes)
HOTEL

a   How is the hotel called? (**What** is … called?)
b   There are many rooms here? (**Are there** …?)
c   Does it have an own bathroom? (… have **its** own bathroom?)
d   Is there a dinner here? (when you ask about meals, you can ask *Can I have dinner here? Is it possible to have dinner here? Does the hotel serve dinner?*)
e   How much does it cost a room? (…**does a room cost?**)

SPORTS CENTRE

f   It has tennis at the sports centre? ('It has' - this is **not** a question form in English. You can say *Does the sports centre have tennis? Has the sports centre got tennis?*)
g   What times can I play tennis? (we use 'what time?' when the answer is, for example, '9 am':
What time does the sports centre open? It opens at 9 am.)
h   There is anything to eat and drink here? (**Is there** anything?)
i   Is it possible a student price? (Look at the correct way to use 'Is it possible?':
<u>Is it possible (+ for someone) + infinitive</u>
Is it possible   (for me)   to get a cheap price?
Is it possible   (for you)   to meet me at 2pm?

TEST TWO
Reading and Writing page 34

Part 1
1 C   2 D   3 G   4 B   5 H

Further Practice and Guidance page 35

Exercise 1

a   You **may** be late if the bus doesn't arrive soon.
b   Sorry, you **mustn't/cannot** smoke inside this office.
c   You **shouldn't** go to that restaurant. It's not very good.
d   After you finish the test, you **can/may** leave if you want to.
e   You **must/have to** show your passport at the check-in desk.
f   We **cannot** go swimming today because the pool is closed!
g   I think you **should** see a doctor if you are ill.

Exercise 2

a   **It's possible that you will** be late if the bus doesn't arrive soon.
b   Sorry, **you are not allowed to** smoke inside this office.

c   **It's not a good idea to** go to that restaurant. It's not very good.
d   After you finish the test, **you are allowed to** leave if you want to.
e   **It is necessary to** show your passport at the check-in desk.
f   **It's not possible** to go swimming today because the pool is closed.
g   **It's a good idea to** see a doctor if you are ill.

Exercise 3
You **have to/must** pay with cash.
Only members **can** play here.
Drivers **should** start their journey early.
You **mustn't/cannot** walk on the grass.
Children under three **mustn't/cannot** play here.
Drivers **shouldn't** forget to lock their cars.
You **can** park here after 5pm and before 9pm.
Students **can** buy cheap fares here.
You **should** buy tickets now.
Customers **must/have to** come back after lunch.
Young children **shouldn't** watch this film.

Part 2
6 A   7 B   8 A   9 C   10 A

Further Practice and Guidance page 38

EXAMPLE: The students finished the test quickly
because it was easy.

Exercise 1

1   take
2   spend
3   pass
4   visit
5   stay
6   go
7   have
8   take
9   make
10 buy
11 send
12 look
13 angry
14 noisy
15 thirsty
16 way
17 road
18 way
19 street
20 road/street
(a road = where people live in house/apartments, or in the countryside)
(a street = where there are shops, or in the city)

Exercise 2

a   taking
b   eat
c   to eat/eat
d   meeting/going
e   to find
f   to call
g   using
h   to visit
i   travelling(AmE traveling)/seeing
j   driving
k   being

Part 3

11 A   12 B   13 B   14 C   15 A

16 B   17 F   18 A   19 C   20 H

Part 4

21 C   22 B   23 B   24 C   25 B   26 A   27 B

Part 5

28 B   29 B   30 A   31 C   32 A   33 A   34 B

35 C

Part 6

36 shower
37 mirror
38 comb
39 toothbrush
40 towel

Further Practice and Guidance page 45

Exercise 1

Shopping	Holidays	Food
Nouns a supermarket a department store an assistant a customer a sale	Nouns a hotel a beach a tourist a passport	Nouns a cooker salt (un.noun) a saucepan a chef /ʃɛf/

Verbs
to buy   – food
            – a present for someone
to spend – (a lot of) money
            – $20
	Verbs
	to reserve – an airplane ticket
	              – a table
	to board – an airplane
	              – a train
		Verbs
		to fry – eggs / onions
		to stir – tea / soup

Adjectives expensive	Adjectives foreign /fɒrɪn/ warm	Adjectives spicy delicious

Exercise 2

1 cheap
2 country/language/food
3 disgusting
4 pepper
5 cooker
6 chef

Part 7

41 to
42 have
43 are
44 where
45 There
46 a
47 before
48 much
49 with
50 it/some

Part 8

51 18 Tower Road, Cardiff (Wales)
52 17 (years old)
53 Canadian
54 Saturday(s)/Sunday(s)
55 shop assistant

Further Practice and Guidance page 50

Language task

Exercise 1

How does the note start? = Hi (name of friend)
How does the note end? = I hope you can come. (Name of writer)
Does the note include the 3 points in the question? = Yes:

1 where the party is - *in our garden*
2 how to travel there - *take the 51 bus from the station/it stops right outside my house.*
3 what to bring - *a few hamburgers*

Exercise 2

1 e   2 f   3 g   4 a   5 h   6 b   7 c   8 d

Exercise 3

1 Let's/could
2 outside/front/on/at
3 Can/don't
4 because/so
5 Would .... like/Would .... like
6 should/suggest
7 could/Could

Exercise 4
1 I'm having
2 on
3 in
4 can
5 the
6 stops
7 a few
8 hope

TEST TWO
Listening page 52

Part 1
1 C   2 C   3 A   4 B   5 C

Further Practice and Guidance page 54

Numbers: Exercise 1b: 13, 40, 15, 60

Dates: Exercise 3b: 16th, 10th, 5th, 22nd, 3rd,
2nd, 20th, 12th, 4th, 15th

Times: Exercise 4
10.00am = ten o'clock/ten a.m.
10.00pm = ten o'clock/ten p.m.
1.00 = one o'clock   1.10 one ten / ten past one
1.15 one fifteen/quarter past one
1.30 one thirty/ half past one
1.40 one forty/twenty to two
1.45 one forty five/quarter to two
1.50 one fifty/ten to two
1.55 one fifty five/five to two

Shapes + Sizes: Exercise 5
Picture 1: a *big*, *square* table with *long* legs.
Picture 2: a *small*, *round* table with *short* legs.

Directions: Exercise 6
It's *on* the table.   It's *opposite* the supermarket.
next to the book.   *past* the library.
under the lamp.   *on* the left.

Part 2
6 F   7 A   8 D   9 C   10 G

Part 3
11 B   12 C   13 A   14 A   15 B

Further Practice and Guidance page 58

11 The question is *Where is the market?*. The speakers
might say **a.** *... in a small road.*
The questions for the other answers might be:
b every Monday and Tuesday = **When** *is the*
market?
c by bus = **How** *did Rita travel to the market?*
d quite large = **What size** *is the market?*

12 The question is *How did Rita travel?* The speakers
might say **a.** *I went by bicycle* or **c.** *Did you get a bus?*
The questions for the other answers might be:
b It's near my house = **Where** *is the market?*
d just ten minutes = **How long** *did it take Rita to go*
to the market?

13 The question is *What did Rita buy?* The speakers
might say **c.** *I got some new shoes.*
I got can mean the same as *I bought.*
The questions for the other answers might be:
a I spent £25 = **How much** *did Rita spend?*

b My cousin came with me = **Who** *went to the*
market with Rita?
d The market was cheap = *What were the* **prices like**
at the market?

14 The question is *How much did she spend?*. The
speakers might say **a.** *I got it for £10* or **d.** *It cost £15*
The questions for the other answers might be:
b Three things for myself = **What** *did Rita buy?*
c The whole afternoon = **How long** *did Rita spend at*
the market?

15 The question is *Who did she meet?* The speakers
might say **b.** *I saw my neighbour at the market* or **c.** *My*
sister was at the market too.
The questions for the other answers might be:
a A friend told me about the market. = **How** *did*
Rita know about the market?
d The bus driver told me where to go. = **How** *did*
Rita find the market?

Part 4
16 door
17 2.45/two forty-five/14.45
18 Welsh
19 412523
20 Tom

Part 5
21 Friday
22 07.30/seven thirty/7.30
23 £4.25
24 newspaper shop
25 camera

TEST TWO
Speaking page 60

Further Practice and Guidance page 61

Part 1
Exercise 1

1 **What do you do?** This is a 'present simple' question.
We use this to ask about what you usually do, for
example: your job, your hobbies, your habits, your
routines, where you live, etc.
Correct answers
a + b: the answers are in present simple: *I go/I work*
d: The speaker uses present continuous in the
answer to show this is *not usual* for her. It is only
something she is doing *now. Usually,* she is a
doctor but *at the moment,* she is studying English.

Wrong answer
c You can say "I work ..." or "I am working ..."
You cannot say "I am work ...".

2 **What did you eat yesterday?** This is a 'past simple'
question. We use this to ask about actions or
situations in the past, for example: what you ate
yesterday, what you did last weekend, etc.
Correct answers
c + d: the answers are in the past simple: *I had/I ate*
b: the answer is in the past simple negative: *I didn't*
have
Wrong answer
a: This is a past continuous sentence. We usually
use past continuous with past simple.

EXAMPLE:
I was eating dinner when   my friend called me.
(past continuous)   (past simple)

3 **Have you travelled to any other countries?** This is a 'present perfect' question. We use this to ask about someone's experience in the past. When you give an answer, you can use present perfect (without exact time). You can also use past simple (with exact time) to give more information.
Correct answers:
a: the answer is in the present perfect:
    I've been   I've been to Argentina and Chile.
d: the answer is in the present perfect/short form answer: *No, I haven't.*
b: the first part of the answer is in the present perfect/short form answer: *Yes, I have.* The second part of the answer is in the past simple and gives more information – the exact time. *I went to Korea last year.*
Wrong answer: I've been to Sweden two years ago.
c: We can't use present perfect (for experience) with an exact time. You can't say *I've been + 2 years ago*

4 **Tell me about your future plans.**
Correct answers:
a: *I want … but I'm not sure it will happen.*
c: the answer is a first conditional sentence: If + present simple form, will + verb
The meaning in this sentence is – *I need to pass my school exams so I can go to university.*
d: *going to + verb:* we use this form to talk about future plans.
Wrong answer:
b: *I go + I have:* this is present simple. We cannot use present simple to talk about future plans.

Exercise 2: Here are some *possible* ways to answer the questions:
1 I'm from + (country)/   I come from + (country)
2 I'm a + (occupation)   I work in/for + (company)
3 I live in + (country/town)
4 I do a lot of sport/read a lot/listen to music/meet my friends.
5 I have a large/small family. I have two younger brothers.
   My mother works for the government.
6 I went to a party/the beach. I met my friends.
   I went shopping.
7 I watched a film on TV.   I went to the gym.
   I cooked dinner for my family.
8 I had a salad for dinner.
   I only had toast for breakfast.   I ate a lot!
9 I started when I was six.
   I began to learn English at Junior High school.
10 I went to the beach every day.   I visited some museums. I took a lot of photographs.
11 Yes, I've been to + (country). No, I haven't.
   Yes. I went to + (country) + in + (year).
12 I'm going to + (verb) …
13 I'm going to …   I want to …
   If I + (present simple), (will) + (verb)

Exercise 3
1 **Correct:** A/B
   Wrong: C *Too much* is always negative, *for example:*

I ate too much food. Now I feel sick. or I spent too much money. Now my wallet is empty!
2 **Correct:** A
   Wrong: B (You need **an object** when you talk about likes and dislikes: *for example*
   Tell me about your job. I love **it**/I enjoy **it**/I like **it**/I dislike **it**/I hate **it**
   C (We use *Yes, I do* with *Do…?* We use *Yes, I am* with *Are you…?*)
3 **Correct:** A
   Wrong: B+C (see 2B+C above)
4 **Correct:** A/B/C
5 **Correct:** A/C
   Wrong: B
   To talk **about** the subject, we use an 'ing' adjective:
   EXAMPLE: subject + be + adjective/ing
   The programme was   boring
   The book   was   interesting
   The film   is   frightening
   To talk about **how we feel** about something, we use an 'ed' adjective:
   EXAMPLE: subject + be + adjective/ed
   I   am   bored   (so I'm going to call my friends)
   John   is   interested (in studying science)
   My sister was frightened (by the film)
6 **Correct:** B The rule is:
   love/enjoy/like/dislike/hate + ing
   for example: "I love mee**ting** new people" "I hate get**ting** up early." I enjoy play**ing** basketball."

Exercise 4
Use the answers to Exercise 3 to help you check your answers to Exercise 4.

Further Practice and Guidance page 64
Part 2

Examiner: Akemi, here is some information about a football match. Nozomi, you don't know anything about the football match, so ask Akemi some questions about it. Now Nozomi, ask Akemi your questions about the football match and Akemi, you answer them.
Nozomi: What is the date of the football match?
Akemi: You mean, when can you see the football match?
Nozomi: Yes.
Akemi: Oh, it's on the 14th March. That's a Saturday.
Nozomi: I see. OK. What teams are there?
Akemi: Teams? Oh, er, England and Scotland. The English team and the Scottish team.
Nozomi: Right. England and Scotland. How much is the cheapest price, please?
Akemi: Price? Do you mean what price are the tickets?
Nozomi: Yes – the cheapest ticket.
Akemi: The cheapest ticket is , er, let me see, £35.
Nozomi: That's not bad. What time does the match start?
Akemi: It starts at 3 o'clock.
Nozomi: 3 o'clock. Alright. And what about the car park?
Akemi: Sorry, can you say that again please?
Nozomi: Yes, I mean, is there a car park near to the football match?

Akemi:	No, there is no parking there. You must come by bus or train.
Nozomi:	Thank you.

Exercise 2
Correct

a   Sorry, I don't understand./Sorry, I didn't understand.
b   Can you say that again?/Can you repeat that?
c   What do you mean?
d   Sorry, I didn't hear you.
e   I didn't catch that./I didn't get what you said.
f   Sorry, what did you say about the cost?/Sorry, what was the cost of that?

Exercise 3

a   "Sorry, <u>what</u> was your name?"
b   "You mean, what time does the train <u>leave</u>?"
c   "Sorry, <u>what</u> time does it close?"
d   "Sorry, <u>how</u> much is the discount?"
e   "Sorry, <u>where</u> is it?"
f   "You mean, what <u>kind</u> of programme?"

TEST THREE
Reading and Writing page 66

Part 1

1 F   2 C   3 G   4 E   5 D

Further Practice and Guidance page 67

Language Task

Exercise 1

In Sue's opinion, the train will be late	True
In line 2, the subject is 'I'	True
In line 2 'expect' is a present simple verb.	True
'I expect there will be a delay' is an active sentence.	True
It is only the station manager who expects the train will be late	False:

he doesn't say 'I expect'. He uses the passive form: 'are expected'. In *this* situation, it suggests that other people (who work for the train company) also expect a delay.

In line 4, the subject is 'delays'.	True
In line 4, 'are expected' is talking about the present.	True
'delays are expected on most trains' is a passive sentence.	True

Exercise 2

1   No photography **is** allowed in **the** exhibition.
2   Hotel reception: **The** door **is** locked at 11.30pm.
3   Lunch **is** served every day **from** 1 – 2pm.
4   Half-price tickets **are sold** after 6pm.
5   **A waitress is wanted in/for the evenings and the weekends.**

Part 2

6 B   7 A   8 C   9 B   10 C

Part 3

11 C   12 B   13 C   14 A   15 C
16 E   17 B   18 G   19 A   20 D

Further Practice and Guidance page 72

Exercise 1

2   someone's plans for the near future
3   someone's emotions or health
4   talking about his plans
5   talking about a problem he has now
6   apologizing
7   the future
8   a fact in the past
9   the length of the film
10 You were good in that game of tennis.
11 someone's emotions or health
12 thank you
13 the meaning of some information
14 "Was the film good?"
15 someone's plans
16 saying 'no' to his friend
17 a past situation
18 complaining to a friend

Exercise 2

1   What <u>do</u> you <u>do</u>?   **B**   I'm <u>a student</u>. (This is my occupation)

2   What <u>are</u> you doing?   **C**   I '<u>m going</u> home. (This is my plan.)

3   How do you <u>feel</u>?   **A**   I'm <u>happy</u>.

4   I <u>hope</u> to go to university.   **B**   I <u>do</u> too. (I also hope to go to university)

5   <u>I've lost</u> my ticket!   **A**   You need to buy another.
(The first speaker lost the ticket in the past and it is still lost now. So she needs another ticket.)

6   I'm sorry <u>I'm late</u>.   **C**   <u>It</u> doesn't matter.
(*It* means *the fact that you are late*. In this situation, *It doesn't matter* means *It is not a problem that you are late.*)

7   <u>Will</u> the plane arrive soon?   **B**   <u>In</u> about ten minutes.   (We can use *in* + a period of time to talk about when something will happen in the future. EXAMPLE: *When are you going on holiday? In about three weeks.*)

8   When <u>did</u> you get here?   **C**   An hour <u>ago</u>
(We only use *ago* for the past/with past simple)

9   <u>How long</u> is the film?   **A**   <u>It lasts</u> two hours.
(We can use the verb *to last* to show how long in time something is.)

10 You <u>played</u> very well.   **A**   You <u>did</u> too. (You also played well)

11 <u>How are you</u>?   **B**   <u>Very well</u>, thanks.

12 That's really <u>kind of you</u>.   **C**   You're <u>welcome</u>.
(We can use *You're welcome* after someone thanks us because we helped them or did something nice for them)

13 What does that mean?   **A**   No idea. (I have no idea/ I don't know)

14 Did you enjoy the film?   **C**   No, not much. (No, I didn't enjoy the film very much)

15 Are you coming with us?   **B**   I don't think <u>so</u>. (No. I don't think I am going with you/ No, I'm not going with you.)

16 I <u>can't lend you any money</u>.   **C**   <u>That's</u> alright. (It's not a problem)

17 Did he damage the car?   A   I'm afraid <u>so</u>. (I'm
                                   afraid = I'm sorry .
                                   so = he <u>did</u> damage
                                   the car)

18 You didn't remember my   B   Sorry about <u>that</u>.
    birthday.   (I'm sorry I didn't
                                   remember your
                                   birthday)

Exercise 3
2 hot/warm
3 Hawaii
4 **b** surprise = because Mark says he doesn't like hot
   places and Hawaii is hot.
5 No, the weather in Hawaii wasn't warm.
6 Hawaii/the mountains
7 Yes, I think you would like Hawaii.
8 The mountain birds and flowers.
9 He offers to show her a video of the mountain birds
   and flowers
10 Canada
11 I didn't know your brother went to Canada.
12 Did your brother go to Canada this year?
13 Yes, he went to Canada last month.
14 Canada.

Part 4
21 C   **22** B   **23** C   **24** B   **25** A   **26** B   **27** C

Part 5
28 C   **29** A   **30** C   **31** B   **32** A   **33** B   **34** C   **35** A

Part 6
36 passport
37 suitcase
38 hotel
39 camera
40 tent

Part 7
41 ago
42 a
43 her
44 It
45 and
46 to
47 took
48 than
49 there
50 of

Further Practice and Guidance page 78

Language task
Exercise 1
1 <u>*are spending*</u> for present time
2 Past simple. ago.
3 *A/an* or *the*. The answer is *a* because Maria is writing
   about the house <u>for the first time</u>.
4 A person : *to stay with <u>me/you/him/her/John</u>* etc. In the
   sentence before, *my grandmother* is the subject.
5 It. (*It* snowed/*It* rained/*It* was sunny/*It* was cold
   etc)
6 and
7 to
8 to take (three hours/a day/a long time) Past.
9 than
10 There
11 of

Exercise 2
Pronouns
1 your/mine/hers
2 There's/it's/it/There
   Use *there* + noun/noun phrase   Use *It* + adjective
3 Everyone/something (or anything)/anything/
   everything/someone/no-one

Verb forms
1 **a** How often <u>do you play</u> tennis? (We use present
       simple for habit and routines.)
   b Usually, <u>I play</u> twice a week.
2 Well, at the moment <u>I'm living</u> with my parents, but
   I want to find my own apartment soon.
   (We use present continuous for present situations +
   actions happening now.)
3 **a** I <u>went</u> to Tokyo last week.
   b Really? Where <u>did you stay</u>? (We use past simple
       for finished actions/situations in the past.)
4 **a** <u>Have you phoned</u> Mr Kitano yet?
       (We use present perfect simple with *yet*: the
       speaker hopes that the other person phoned Mr
       Kitano sometime in the past. The exact past time
       is not important to the speaker. The important
       thing is that the phone call happened.)
   b Yes, I <u>spoke</u> to him 10 minutes ago.
       (We use past simple with *ago*. This tells us
       exactly when the phone call happened.)
   c He <u>is coming</u> to London next week.
       (We can use present continuous for future time –
       for future arrangements.)
5 Yes. I <u>was waiting</u> for the bus when the truck
   crashed into the shop.
   (We use past continuous to show that this action
   started before a second action.)
   I was waiting (past continuous) happens before *the
   truck crashed* (past simple).
6 Yes, <u>I'm going to visit</u> some friends.
   (We use *going to* + verb for future plans.)
7 Yes. I think <u>I'll</u> go to bed early tonight.
   (We use *will* + verb when we decide something
   (about the future) <u>now</u>. We often use *I think* + *I will*
   for sudden decisions.)
8 The instructions <u>are written</u> in German.
   (This is a passive sentence. We don't know <u>who</u>
   wrote the instructions. You can say *The students <u>are</u>
   <u>writing</u> in German* but not *The instructions are writing
   in German.*)

Modals
1 Can/Could/Would
2 shall/should
3 may
4 should/could
5 have to/need to/must
6 need

Connectives
I passed my driving test
and my English exam!
but I don't have any money to buy a car!
because I had a lot of driving lessons.

You could come to the café with us –
when you finish work.
or you could go with Jane.
and have a coffee there.

Please visit me and my family –
if you come to Seoul.
because my mother really wants to meet you!
but don't come in May.

I'm planning to go to New Zealand –
when I graduate this year.
where my cousins live.
or Australia next year.

Articles
1 a
2 the
3 the
4 a
5 a
6 the
7 the
8 the
9 the
10 the
11 the
12 the
13 a

Part 8
51 22 Kings Road
52 19
53 Australian
54 Friday(s)
55 (in) Today Magazine

Further Practice and Guidance page 82
Exercise 1
How does the email start? = Dear (Name of friend)
How does the email end? = Love (Name of sender)
Does the email include the 3 points in the question? = Yes
1 what is the weather like? = *It is hot and sunny*
2 where are you staying? = *in a lovely hotel near the beach*
3 tell me how you are spending your time. = *swimming in the morning and diving in the afternoon*

Exercise 2
Beginning a note/an email
good ways to begin: To Peter, Dear Peter, Hi Peter, Peter,
wrong: Dear friend
business letter: Dear Peter Jones,
Ending a note/an email
business letter: yours sincerely, Claudia
the end of an invitation: I hope you can come! Claudia
the end of a letter making an arrangement: See you soon Claudia

Exercise 3
Describing the weather
a warm/hot/boiling
   chilly/cold/freezing
   dry/wet
   sunny/cloudy
b snowing/raining/shining
c storm

Places to stay

	in the city	at the beach	in the country-side	in the mountains	near the motorway	someone can cook all your meals for you	this can be quite cheap	the family who own this often live and work here	you might share a room with people you don't know
four star hotel	✓	✓	✓	✓		✓			
motel	✓				✓			✓	
ski-lodge				✓		✓			✓
campsite		✓	✓				✓		
backpacker's hostel	✓		✓	✓			✓		✓
pension		✓		✓			✓	✓	
bed and breakfast		✓	✓	✓			✓	✓	

Things to do on holiday
1 go sightseeing
2 buy a souvenir
3 play tennis
4 go walking in the mountains/forest around the town/city
5 buy/write postcards
6 go shopping
7 visit museums
8 go sailing
9 try new food
10 go diving
11 take photographs
12 go swimming
13 play volleyball
14 go horse-riding

TEST THREE
Listening page 84

Part 1
1 B   2 B   3 C   4 B   5 A

Part 2
6 D   7 E   8 A   9 G   10 C

Part 3
11 C   12 B   13 B   14 A   15 A

Part 4
16 (the) airport
17 7am/07.00/7 o'clock in the morning
18 Linden
19 286013
20 Peter

Part 5
21 Saturday
22 ticket office
23 (£)3.50
24 drinks
25 (a/the) market

Further Practice and Guidance page 89

Exercise 2
a   Peter **Rees**
b   Simon **Hughes**
c   Jane **Thatcher**
d   Julie **Harding**
e   Andrew **Finch**
f   Emily **Dickson**
g   Steven **Elliot**

Exercise 3
a   12 **Vauxhall** Road
b   44 **Grafton** Avenue
c   6 **Tudor** Street
d   81 **Drury** Avenue
e   16 **Edinburgh** Street
f   158 **Dominion** Road

TEST THREE
Speaking page 90

Further Practice and Guidance page 91

Part 1
Ways to explain what you mean:
Example 1: I study, er, hotel management. I have to think about, er, <u>who works at the hotel, the advertising, the money that the hotel needs</u>.
Example 2: it was <u>too quiet</u>. I mean, <u>there were not many things to do there</u>.
Example 3: <u>I don't know how you say it, but</u> the Brazilian people have a special party – everyone dances, everyone wears something special.

Further Practice and Guidance page 93

Part 2
Joy: Takeshi, what is **the** name of the language school?
Takeshi: It **is** called the Swan Language School.
Joy: Can I study~~ing~~ all languages here?
Takeshi: No, there ~~is~~ **are** only courses in English, German, Spanish & French.
Joy: When **are** the lessons ~~are~~?
Takeshi: The lessons are in the daytime and in the evening, six days a week.
Joy: Does the school have good teacher**s**?
Takeshi: Yes, the teachers are excellent.
Joy: And ~~how~~ **what** is the address of the school?
Takeshi: It's 10 Station Road, Bridgetown.
Joy: Thank you.

TEST FOUR
Reading and Writing page 94

Part 1
1 F   2 D   3 H   4 E   5 G

Part 2
6 A   7 C   8 B   9 B   10 A

Part 3
11 B   12 B   13 C   14 A   15 A
16 F   17 H   18 D   19 B   20 G

Part 4
21 A   22 C   23 A   24 B   25 B   26 A   27 C

Further Practice and Guidance page 98

Comprehension task

1   15. So – he is not a <u>young</u> child.

2   '<u>Only</u> after a year' suggests that the course is longer/the course is more than one year.
The four words are: <u>without getting his diploma.</u>

3   No. We only know that Juan and Antonio met there. Perhaps Antonio was in the audience or a friend introduced them.

4   No. The text tells us that people from many countries saw this film. The text suggests that Hollywood film-makers saw the film and they thought Juan was a good actor – so - the film-makers asked him to come to Hollywood.

5   Yes, Juan spoke English in The King, but he didn't understand the meaning of the English words he was saying. The important phrase is '<u>he had no idea</u>' what any of them (the English words) meant.

6   <u>Juan</u> decided he needed to learn English – probably because he wanted a career in Hollywood.
It was difficult for him to learn languages: the text says '<u>he was never good at languages</u>'.
We know that Juan did <u>not</u> teach himself because the text says '<u>he went back to school</u>' to learn English.

7 *career* and *enjoys.*

8 No. The last two sentences in paragraph five only tell us what Juan wants to do <u>in the future</u>. The text doesn't tell us what Juan prefers.

Part 5

28 A   29 B   30 A   31 C   32 C   33 A
34 C   35 B

Part 6

36 pilot
37 dentist
38 journalist
39 taxi driver
40 artist

Part 7

41 in
42 not
43 me
44 at
45 have
46 will
47 a
48 did
49 There
50 went

Part 8

51 Mike Green
52 7.30pm
53 Photographing Animals
54 DVD player
55 (a) map

Further Practice and Guidance page 103

Comprehension task

1 Tim Harris and Rachel belong to the Camera Club. Mike Green is just a visitor.
2 He'll be here at …
3 speak/Mike Green will speak about <u>Photographing Animals</u>./Yes, you need to use capital letters.
4 an object/noun
5 post

Exercise 1

Country	Nationality	Language
Someone from France	is **French** /	speaks **French**
Someone from Germany	is **German** /	speaks **German**
Someone from Italy	is **Italian** /	speaks **Italian**
Someone from **Greece**	is Greek /	speaks Greek
Someone from Australia	is **Australian** /	speaks **English**
Someone from **Poland**	is Polish /	speaks Polish
Someone from Japan	is **Japanese** /	speaks **Japanese**
Someone from the USA	is **American** /	speaks **English**
Someone from Brazil	is **Brazilian** /	speaks **Portuguese**

Exercise 2

a teacher
b journalist
c dentist
d sales assistant
e banker
f doctor
g manager
h police officer

Exercise 3

a The class starts at **5pm** etc
  on **Monday** etc
  in **October** etc

b The flight leaves at **5pm** etc
  from **Heathrow airport** etc
  takes **3 hours** etc

Exercise 4

> 43 Cranwell Rd
> Muswell Hill
> London
>
> The Manager   2nd February 2005
> The Queen Elizabeth Hotel
> 1 High Street
> Oxford
>
> Dear Mr Fisher
>
> I stayed at your hotel from Monday 25th January to Wednesday 27th. Unfortunately, I left a valuable book in my room. It is called History of the Americas and it is written in Spanish.
>
> Please send it to me and I will pay for the postage.
>
> Yours sincerely
>
> Dr Anna Atkins

TEST FOUR
Listening page 106

Part 1
1 B   2 A   3 C   4 A   5 C

Part 2
6 F   7 B   8 D   9 H   10 G

Part 3
11 A   12 C   13 B   14 B   15 A

Part 4
16 Woods
17 single
18 (£)65
19 dinner
20 WL02 FTR

Part 5
21 fishing
22 1.15
23 (£)2
24 postcards
25 maps

Further Practice and Guidance page 110

Exercise 1
/g/ flight <u>single</u> daughter <u>luggage</u>
/p/ <u>stamp</u> cupboard psychiatrist receipt
/d/ grandmother sandwich Wednesday <u>midnight</u>

Exercise 2
a ca<u>s</u>tle
b i<u>s</u>land
c autum<u>n</u>
d clim<u>b</u>
e li<u>s</u>ten
e sa<u>l</u>mon
f lam<u>b</u>

TEST FOUR
Speaking page 111

Further Practice and Guidance page 112

Part 2
Anna and Eva probably do enough to pass the KET
Speaking paper, but they could get better marks.

- if Anna gives full answers:

2 weeks. August 1ˢᵗ to August 15ᵗʰ.
It's for 2 weeks, from August 1ˢᵗ to August 15ᵗʰ.
The campsite is near mountains and river.
The campsite is near some mountains and a river.
Oh, er, campsite shop. There is food and drink.
You can buy food and drink from the campsite shop.
Nevis Holidays has more information. 5543026.
If you want more information, you can call Nevis
    Holidays. The phone number is 5543026.

- if Eva responds more naturally:

Sometimes Eva says 'Yes' and sometimes she just asks
    another question.
It is better for Eva to say 'I see' or 'OK' or 'Alright' or
    'That's good' etc
It is also not natural to say 'I finished' at the end of a
    conversation.
Eva could say 'Thank you' or 'That's great' to finish the
    conversation.

- if they explain things more clearly:

Anna does not understand Eva's question *'Is there a shop
    nearby?'* Eva repeats the same question. It is more
    helpful if Eva asks the question in a different way:
EXAMPLE:
Is there a shop near the campsite?
Can I do some shopping at the campsite?

LISTENING SCRIPTS

KET PRACTICE TEST 1

TEST ONE PART ONE

Example.

How many people were at the party?

Man: Were there many people at Mary's party?
Woman: Thirty
Man: That's a lot.
Woman: Yes, but she's got a large house.

1   What time is the girl's appointment?

Boy: Are you going to the dentist's in the morning?
Girl: Yes. I wanted to go at nine-thirty, but they only had appointments at either ten o'clock or ten-thirty.
Boy: But your class starts at ten-thirty.
Girl: I know. So I'm going at ten. But it should be OK.

2   How far is the nearest petrol station?

Woman: Excuse me, is Wellstown far from here?
Man: It's about ten kilometres away.
Woman: Is there a petrol station on the way?
Man: There's one about two kilometres down this road on the left and another four kilometres away on the main road.

3   What did Monica do at the weekend?

Boy: Hi Monica. Did you have a good time cycling at the weekend?
Monica: Well, I didn't go cycling in the end. My friend has just bought a new sports car, so we went out in that.
Boy: Really? That sounds fun.
Monica: Yes, it was just like the one in the advertisement on television.

4   Which fruit does the woman buy?

Woman: I'd like to buy some fruit, please? Have you got any bananas?
Man: Sorry. I've got some very nice apples or some oranges, but I've sold all my bananas.
Woman: It's OK, oranges will be fine. One kilo please. I've already got some apples at home.
Man: Thank you.

5   Where is the man going next year?

Woman: And do you have to travel to other countries as part of your job?
Man: Yes. I went to China last month and next year I'm going to Japan.
Woman: Oh you are lucky. And have you been to Thailand yet?
Man: Oh yes. I've been three times actually.

TEST ONE PART TWO

David: Tina, come in.
Tina: Thanks David – What a beautiful flat! Where did you get all these things?

David: Well, my father bought the CD player, and the other things were presents from my family too. My brother gave me that red sofa. It was in his flat with two red chairs, but it was too big. He's still got the chairs.
Tina: And what about the table that the CD player's on?
David: My sister gave me that. She bought a new table and chairs when she got married. This is her old one.
Tina: And this desk looks really old.
David: Yeah, it was my grandfather's desk when he was a student. He gave me that and my grandmother gave me that mirror over there on the wall next to the lamp.
Tina: And what about your mother?
David: She bought me those bookshelves. My brother helped me put them on the wall. We put the mirror up at the same time.
Tina: It all looks really nice.

TEST ONE PART THREE

Woman: Hello? Video shop.
Gary: Hello. My name's Gary. Where is the video shop please?
Woman: In the city centre – next to the train station.
Gary: OK. How much does it cost to join?
Woman: It costs five pounds to join and then two pounds a day for each video you take home. You pay one pound fifty for returning a video late.
Gary: Do you have the latest films?
Woman: New films arrive every week. Every month, we send out a list of new films. Once a year, there's a video club meeting – people tell us what they'd like in future.
Gary: What do people ask for?
Woman: American films mostly– and we have lots of those. But we also have some good British films and also a few from Australia.
Gary: When's the shop open?
Woman: From eight o'clock in the morning till seven in the evening, Monday to Saturday. We're also open Sunday mornings, from 10 till 12.
Gary: Right. I'd like to join.
Woman: OK. You need to fill in a form. They have them in the shop, or I can send you one by post, or there's one on the club's website.
Gary: I'm going shopping later. I'll come in and get one then. Thank you very much.
Woman: Goodbye.

TEST ONE PART FOUR

Gavin: Hello, can you help me. I'd like to take a course here.
Woman: Certainly. Could I have your name, please?
Gavin: It's Gavin Lake.
Woman: How do you spell your surname?
Gavin: L.A.K.E
Woman: Thank you. Now which course would you like to do?
Gavin: I'd like to learn a language.

Woman: Right. We've got French, Spanish, Russian, Japanese …
Gavin: I did French last year. It was very good, but I'd like to do something different this year. When does the Russian course start?
Woman: The next language courses start on January the sixth, but that's Spanish and Japanese, and, oh yes, Russian begins on the twelfth.
Gavin: So is it every Wednesday evening?
Woman: No lessons are on Tuesdays and Saturdays. You can choose.
Gavin: Oh Tuesdays are better for me. I play football on Saturdays. So, how much does the course cost?
Woman: It's three pounds fifty per lesson, then seven pounds fifty for the book and homework CD.
Gavin: Oh yes that's fine …

TEST ONE PART FIVE

Woman: Good afternoon shoppers. Welcome to Newman's Supermarket. Here is some information about special things happening in the shop today.

First - Buy your eggs here today and we will give you a free book which tells you how to make beautiful cakes and biscuits. You can find the eggs at the back of the shop near the milk and fruit juices.

Next, something at a very special price. We have some very good Swiss chocolate which usually costs four pounds fifty for 100 grams. But today you can buy it for only two pounds twenty five for 100 grams. You can find this bargain near the entrance.

Also, why not stay and have lunch with us in the restaurant. There is a wide range of sandwiches, including chicken, cheese and fish or perhaps you would like to try our soup. Each day there is a different soup in the restaurant and today it is tomato. That's in the restaurant.

Finally, you can win a free television if you enter our competition today. Just fill in your name and telephone number on the special card and put it in the box at the cash desk.

Thank you for shopping at Newman's.

KET PRACTICE TEST 2

TEST TWO PART ONE

Example.
Man: Were there many people at Mary's party?
Woman: Thirty
Man: That's a lot.
Woman: Yes, but she's got a large house.

1 What type of soup does Paul choose?

Woman: Hello. Can I help you?
Man: Yes, I'd like some hot soup please. Have you got onion soup?
Woman: Not today, I'm afraid, and the tomato soup has all gone, so we've only got chicken soup left.
Man: I'll have some of that then … I had tomato soup yesterday, anyway.

2 What time does the play start?

Woman: Don't forget we're going to the theatre tonight. What time do you finish work?
Man: Oh not until six o'clock. Will we have time for something to eat?
Woman: Yes plenty of time. The play starts at seven forty-five. Let's meet for a pizza at about six - fifteen.
Man: Oh yes. That's a good idea.

3 What is Ben going to do tonight?

Girl: Are you going to watch the football on television tonight, Ben?
Ben: I can't. I've got too much homework to do.
Girl: Really? We're all going to the disco afterwards. We could see you there.
Ben: I'm sorry, but I can't tonight.

4 How much will the woman pay for the coffee?

Woman: I'd like a cup of coffee, please.
Man: Do you want a large cup at one ninety-five, a medium at one seventy-five or a small one at one fifty?
Woman: Oh. Medium, please.
Man: Thank you.

5 Which mirror will they buy?

Woman: Oh look at these beautiful mirrors. Look there's one that looks like a star.
Man: Oh I don't like that one. And I think the square one is better than the round one.
Woman: Yes, you're right. Let's buy it.
Man: OK.

TEST TWO PART TWO

Fiona: Oh Dad, everyone in my class knows the job they want to do in the future.
Father: Do they, Fiona?
Fiona: Yes. John's only interested in sport, but he knows that he wants to play football for a top team.
Father: Really? And the others?
Fiona: Well Suzie's father is a doctor, but she wants to be a film star. She's very pretty, but she can't act.
Father: And Bob – does he want to be a teacher like his brother?
Fiona: Bob's really good at drawing and painting, but he doesn't want to be an art teacher, he wants to be a real artist.
Father: And Mary – the farmer's daughter?
Fiona: She's taking flying lessons because she wants to fly planes round the world for a big airline.
Father: Well that's a surprise. Doesn't David want to be a pilot?
Fiona: No, David wants to work on a farm.
Father: Really! So does anybody want to be a journalist like me?
Fiona: Anna wrote an article for the school magazine. She'd like to work on a newspaper.
Father: So what about you, Fiona?
Fiona: I don't know.

TEST TWO PART THREE

Rita: Brian. I've found a really good street market.
Brian: Have you, Rita?
Rita: Yes, I went on Wednesday. I know you work then, but you could go on Saturday, and it's there on Mondays too.
Brian: So, where is it?
Rita: Well you go down North Street and the market's in a small road on the left. It's called Hill Street, and at the other end is Wood Street.
Brian: But that's a long way. Did you get a bus?
Rita: No, the bus doesn't go that way. I went by bicycle, but it wouldn't cost much in a taxi.
Brian: So what did you buy?
Rita: Well, I wanted a music CD or a video, but they didn't have any I wanted. But I got a really interesting book about film stars instead.
Brian: And was it cheap?
Rita: Well, it costs seven pounds fifty usually, and I've seen it for four pounds fifty in the shops – but I got it for three pounds fifty.
Brian: That's good.
Rita: I saw my neighbour there too. She was taking her cousin to see the dentist in the next street. She goes there a lot and thinks it's a very good market.

TEST TWO PART FOUR

Man: Hello. Washing Machine Repairs. Can I help you?
Angela: Oh yes, my name's Angela White and my washing machine is broken.
Man: I see. And what's wrong with your machine.
Angela: The door doesn't work, so I can't open it. The water has all gone, but my clothes are still inside. Can you come and repair it, please?
Man: Yes, of course. Are you at home all day?
Angela: I'm at work now, but I will be at home any time after two - fifteen.
Man: Right. I can send someone at two forty five – is that all right?
Angela: Yes, that's good, because the children are at school until three - fifteen.
Man: What's the address, please?
Angela: 24 Welsh Street. That's W.E. L. S. H. street.
Man: Oh yes, I know. It's near Park Road.
Angela: Yes that's right. And my phone number is 412523.
Man: That's good. The repair man will phone if he's going to be late. His name is Tom, and he will be in a white van. Can he park at your house?
Angela: Oh yes, no problem.
Man: Good. Thank you for calling.
Angela: Thank you.

TEST TWO PART FIVE

Teacher: I've come to tell you about the coach trip to Manchester, one of the largest cities in England. Now usually, we go on coach trips on Thursday. But this week we're going on Friday instead. I hope that's alright for everybody.

It's a long way to Manchester, so the coach will leave at 7.30 from outside the college. Don't be late. We'll come back at about eight o'clock in the evening, but it could be later if the roads are busy.

The cost of the trip is usually five twenty-five for adults, but students can go for only four pounds twenty-five, which is a very good price. So buy your ticket soon to be sure of a place. Now, I don't sell the tickets. You have to go to the newspaper shop to buy one.

And I almost forgot. Don't bring any lunch with you. We'll give you free sandwiches and fruit juice on the coach. But don't forget to bring your camera. It's a beautiful city and you'll want to take lots of photographs. Have a good time!

KET PRACTICE TEST 3

TEST THREE PART ONE

Example.

Man: Were there many people at Mary's party?
Woman: Thirty
Man: That's a lot.
Woman: Yes, but she's got a large house.

1   What does the woman want to drink?

Man: I need something to drink. Shall we stop for a cup of tea?
Woman: I'd prefer a cold drink.
Man: OK. Let's go and get a glass of fruit juice at that café.
Woman: A bottle of water will be fine for me.

2   Which woman is the new maths teacher?

Boy: That's your new maths teacher, isn't it?
Girl: No, my teacher has got short hair, but it isn't blond like hers.
Boy: Oh yes. I made a mistake.
Girl: And she never wears glasses. I think that's Mrs Black over there, the new history teacher.

3   What did the boy see at the zoo?

Woman: Did you enjoy going to the zoo?
Boy: The monkeys were really funny. But we didn't have time to see the lions.
Woman: I like watching the elephants.
Boy: Oh, the elephant house was closed.

4   How does the man travel to work?

Woman: Is your journey to work easier, now you've changed your job?
Man: Yes, it's much better. I don't miss the journey on the train at all.
Woman: Do you take the bus now?
Man: There is a bus, but I always take my bike. It's quicker when there's a lot of traffic.

5   What is the date of the concert?

Girl: Are you coming to my school concert. It's in February.
Man: I don't know, I'm afraid – I'm going on a business trip on the ninth.
Girl: It's on the fifth, just before the half-term holiday begins.

Man: Oh yes, that starts on the seventh, doesn't it. That's good then. I'll be here for the concert.

TEST THREE PART TWO

Maria: Hello Tom. Come in.
Tom: Hi Maria, oh your house looks very different since the last time I was here.
Maria: Yes, I've painted almost every room. I used my favourite colour, pink, in the hall. I really like it. Do you remember, the living room was orange? It was horrible, so I painted it yellow. It goes with my sofas.
Tom: I thought all the rooms would be pink!
Maria: No, come and see the dining room. The walls were blue and green squares. So I painted it all the same colour.
Tom: It's a very nice blue. Isn't it the same colour as your kitchen?
Maria: I've got a new wooden floor in the kitchen. So I chose a very light brown for the walls.
Tom: Have you painted upstairs?
Maria: Yes, my bedroom furniture is pink, so I used a light purple for the walls. And the bathroom was the same orange colour as downstairs. I chose white because I didn't really know what colour to paint it.
Tom: Well, I think you've worked really hard.

TEST THREE PART THREE

Man: Toy Shop.
Sonia: Hello. My name's Sonia. I saw an advertisement for a new game. I think it's called *Go*.
Man: Sorry, I don't know it. Ah … there's a new game called *Start*.
Sonia. That's the one I mean. I'm sorry, my mistake. Do you sell it?
Man: Yes. We only have a few left this week, because we've nearly sold them all in the two weeks since we got them.
Sonia: Is the game only for four players?
Man: I think you need two people or more. It's not a game for only one person.
Sonia: Can anyone play this game? My sister's only five.
Man: It is for people under the age of sixteen. But it wouldn't be interesting for children younger than 8 – it takes quite a long time to play.
Sonia: How long is one game?
Man: The idea is you have a board which shows different countries. You travel round the world and try to collect more cards than the other players in an hour. The person who has the most after that time, wins the game.
Sonia: I see.
Man: There's a competition with the game at the moment. The prize is a trip to America for only five pounds.
Sonia: Great. Thanks.
Man: That's alright.

TEST THREE PART FOUR

Woman: Hello. ABC Taxi Company.
Harry: Hello. My name's Harry Todd. I'd like to book a taxi.

Woman: Certainly, Mr Todd. Where would you like to go?
Harry: I've got to meet a friend from Italy at the airport, but my car is at the garage at the moment.
Woman: OK, the airport. Is that tomorrow?
Harry: No, the day after.
Woman: OK, Saturday, then. What time?
Harry: Her plane lands at 8am, so I'll need to leave the house at seven. I don't want to be late.
Woman: That's no problem. We'll have a driver at your house at that time. What's your address, please?
Harry: 39 Linden Road, that's L.I.N.D.E.N road.
Woman: Oh yes, at the top of City Road.
Harry: That's right. And my phone number is 286013.
Woman: That's fine. The taxi driver will call you if he can't find your house. The driver will be Peter. It'll be about £25.
Harry: Alright. Thanks.
Woman: OK. Thanks for calling.

TEST THREE PART FIVE

Woman: Hello everyone. I'd like to give you some information about the boat trip. We didn't have a trip last Wednesday because of exams, so we're going on a special trip on Saturday. I hope you can all come.

The boat leaves at ten-thirty, so we'll meet at ten. Please don't be late because the boat gets very full. We normally meet here at the college when we go on trips, but you all know River Street, don't you? I'll be at the ticket office to meet you there.

The trip usually costs four pounds fifty for adults, but you're all students, so it's only three pounds fifty. It's very cheap – the boat trip takes three hours.

Now, on the boat, drinks are available and they're not expensive, but you will need to bring some food for lunch.

The boat will stop at several beautiful places so please bring your cameras. It will also stop at Hamble Village for an hour and we'll get out to look at the market which is just by the river. I think it will be a great day!

KET PRACTICE TEST 4

TEST FOUR PART ONE

Example.
Man: Were there many people at Mary's party?
Woman: Thirty
Man: That's a lot.
Woman: Yes, but she's got a large house.

1 How much will the man pay for the jacket?
Woman: This is a nice jacket. And it's the right size for you.
Man: Sixty-five pounds is too much.
Woman: OK, try this one. It's only thirty-five pounds.

Man: I don't like the colour. Here's one for forty-five pounds. I'll take that.

2 Where did the woman have lunch?

Man: Annie, do you want to have lunch with us today? We're going for a picnic.
Woman: Sorry, I've got to take my car to the garage.
Man: You should eat something.
Woman: Don't worry. I had a sandwich at the café near the park.

3 What is the girl's favourite subject at school?

Boy: That was a good lesson! I like the new History teacher.
Girl: She's very nice, much friendlier than the teacher we had last year. But the subject's so boring. I like Geography best.
Boy: Science is my favourite.
Girl: Oh, I really hate Science. I never understand it.

4 How will the man travel to London?

Woman: Why don't you fly to London? It's very cheap now.
Man: Yes, I tried to book a seat on the plane. There weren't any left so I decided to go by train – it's two hours quicker than the coach.
Woman: Was the ticket expensive?
Man: No, I got a special price. It didn't cost much more than the coach.

5 Which shop will they go to next?

Boy: Can we go home now?
Girl: I've just got to look in one more shop.
Boy: But we've spent all afternoon looking at clothes. I'm tired. And we've been in more than five shoe shops.
Girl: I need a birthday present for my little sister. I'll just go into this shop and buy her a game. Then we can go home.

TEST FOUR PART TWO

Jack: Did you make all this food, Helena? It looks great!
Helena: No, Jack. Everybody bought in some food, you were the only one I asked to bring drinks. Thanks a lot for bringing them by the way. Do you know Suzie made that pizza herself. You should try a piece.
Jack: I will. And who made that chocolate cake, the one behind the sandwiches?
Helena: Julie brought that. I think she said her Mum made it.
Jack: I love sweet things. I see that Mark's here. Did he bring anything?
Helena: I asked him to bring some fruit or biscuits. He just brought biscuits. He said he never eats fruit.
Jack: I suppose you made the salad, Helena.
Helena: No, my job was to organize the music and the lights. I asked Tim to bring it. I think he bought it from the supermarket, but it looks ok.
Jack: And what about Sally?

Helena: I said she could bring anything she wanted, so she brought that big bowl of sweets. Mark helped her to choose them.
Jack: Well, I'm hungry. Can I have a sandwich?

TEST FOUR PART THREE

Woman: Hello.
Martin: Hello. My name's Martin. Could you tell me about the job for a kitchen assistant?
Woman: Yes, I need someone to work for six weeks in the holidays.
Martin: Where is the job?
Woman: Near Azco Supermarket – opposite the City Hotel, there's a café called Lunchstop – that's us.
Martin: I'm free to work between fifteen and twenty hours a week. How many hours is this job?
Woman: It's for twenty hours a week, twelve of those will be in the evenings.
Martin: How much is the pay?
Woman: All our kitchen assistants get the same pay. Actually it's just gone up from five pounds to five pounds fifty.
Martin: Oh, that's good. Can I eat my meals there?
Woman: Kitchen assistants can get cheaper meals. Also, because you have work late at the weekends, we pay for a taxi to take you home after work.
Martin: It sounds interesting. Can I come and meet you?
Woman: Yes, I'm busy on Saturday. I can see you next Monday or Thursday at ten o'clock …
Martin: I'll come on Monday then. Thanks.

TEST FOUR PART FOUR

David: Hello, can you help me. I'd like to book a room for tonight.
Woman: Certainly. Could I have your name, please?
David: It's David Woods.
Woman: How do you spell your surname?
David: W.O.O.D.S.
Woman: Thank you. You've stayed here before, haven't you?
David: Yes, that's right.
Woman: Now, would you like a double, a single or a twin room?
David: I don't really need a double room this time. My wife is staying at home. Have you got a quiet twin or single room?
Woman: The twin rooms are all full tonight, but I can give you a single on the third floor.
David: That's great. How much will that cost? I think I paid eighty pounds last time.
Woman: That was for a larger room. The price is normally seventy pounds for this room, but we'll let you have it for sixty-five pounds, as you've stayed here before.
David: Thanks. I don't want to have breakfast tomorrow morning, but is your restaurant open tonight? I'd like dinner.
Woman: Yes, that's fine. One other thing, have you parked in the hotel car park?
David: Yes, my number plate is W L 0 2 F T R.
Woman: That's fine, thanks...

TEST FOUR PART FIVE

Woman: Welcome to Wexford History Museum. I'd like to tell you a little about the museum before you start your visit. It opened in 1923, and the building we're in was once an old school. During your visit you will learn all about the history of fishing. Some of the things in the museum are over three thousand years old.

Our guides will be happy to give you a tour. The twelve-fifteen tour has nearly finished, but there's a tour at one-fifteen, and another one at two-fifteen. They're every hour until five-fifteen. It doesn't cost anything to look round the museum by yourself, and it's only two pounds each for the tour.

Now, I'm sure you'll enjoy a visit to our shop, which sells lots of lovely things. For those of you who are on holiday in Wexford, you can buy postcards here. If you need any stamps or envelopes, the post-office is just next to the museum. Our shop also has books on many subjects – history, language, cooking, plants and birds – and there are maps as well. You'll certainly find lots of ideas for presents.

Enjoy your visit today.

Further Practice and Guidance
Test 2 Numbers Exercise 1a

How do you pronounce these numbers?

3	13	30
4	14	40
5	15	50
6	16	60

Further Practice and Guidance
Test 2 Numbers Exercise 1b

Circle the numbers from Exercise 1a that you hear.

13   40   15   60

Further Practice and Guidance
Test 2 Numbers Exercise 1c

How do you pronounce these numbers?

33	303	333
55	505	555

Further Practice and Guidance
Test 2 Prices Exercise 2

How do you pronounce these prices?

$50	£50	£55	£505	£550
£2.10	£8.15	£10.99	£5.75	£4.30

Further Practice and Guidance
Test 2 Dates Exercise 3a

How do you pronounce these dates?

1st of May	2nd of January
3rd of October	4th of June

Further Practice and Guidance
Test 2 Dates Exercise 3b

Circle the dates that you hear.

Sixteenth	Tenth
Fifth	Twenty-second
Third	Second
Twentieth	Twelfth
Fourth	Fifteenth

Further Practice and Guidance
Test 2 Times Exercise 4

How do you pronounce these times?

10.00 am	10.00 pm
1.00	1.10
1.15	1.30
1.40	1.45
1.50	1.55

Further Practice and Guidance
Test 3 Paper 2 Part 4 Exercise 1

A	B	C	D	E	F	G	H	I	J
K	L	M	N	O	P	Q	R	S	T
U	V	W	X	Y	Z				

Further Practice and Guidance
Test 3 Paper 2 Part 4 Exercise 2

Peter Rees. That's R-double e-s
Simon Hughes. That's H-u-g-h-e-s
Jane Thatcher. That's T-h-a-t-c-h-e-r
Julie Harding. That's H-a-r-d-i-n-g
Andrew Finch. That's F-i-n-c-h
Emily Dickson. That's D-i-c-k-s-o-n
Steven Elliot. That's E-double l-i-o-t

Further Practice and Guidance
Test 3 Paper 2 Part 4 Exercise 3

12 Vauxhall Rd. That's V-a-u-x-h-a-double l
44 Grafton Avenue. That's G-r-a-f-t-o-n
6 Tudor Street. That's T-u-d-o-r
81 Drury Avenue. That's D-r-u-r-y
16 Edinburgh Street. That's E-d-i-n-b-u-r-g-h
158 Dominion Rd. That's D-o-m-i-n-i-o-n

Further Practice and Guidance
Test 4 Paper 2 Part 5 Pronunciation and listening task Exercise 1

flight	single
daughter	luggage
stamp	cupboard
psychiatrist	receipt
grandmother	sandwich
Wednesday	midnight

Further Practice and Guidance
Test 4 Paper 2 Part 5 Pronunciation and listening task Exercise 2

castle	island
autumn	climb
listen	salmon
lamb	

CD 1
TEST ONE

CD 2
TEST THREE

Further Practice and Guidance

TEST FOUR

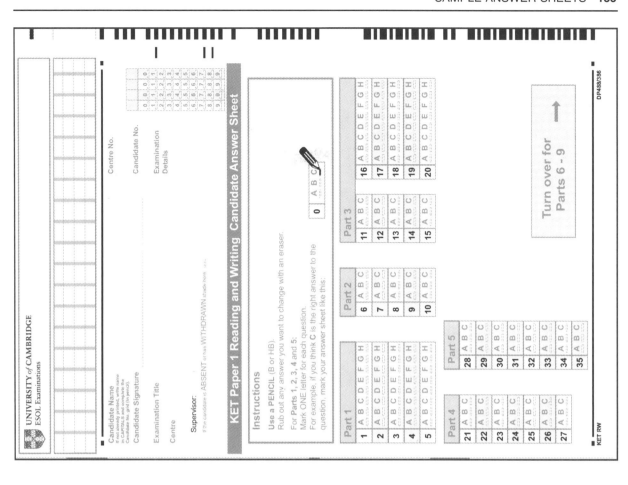

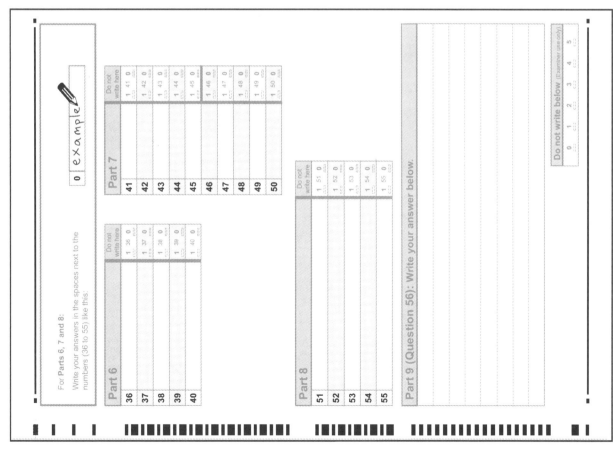

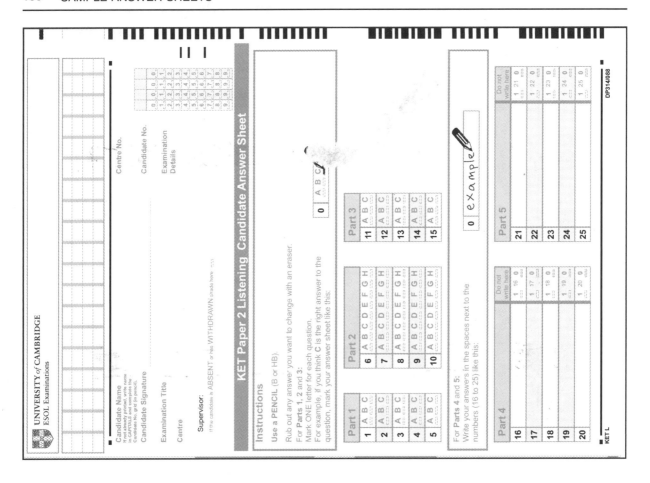

UNIVERSITY *of* CAMBRIDGE
ESOL Examinations

Candidate Name
If not already printed, write name
in CAPITALS and complete the
Candidate No. grid (in pencil).

Candidate Signature

Examination Title

Centre

Supervisor:
If the candidate is ABSENT or has WITHDRAWN shade here

Centre No.

Candidate No.

Examination
Details

KET Paper 2 Listening Candidate Answer Sheet

Instructions

Use a PENCIL (B or HB).

Rub out any answer you want to change with an eraser.
For Parts 1, 2 and 3:
Mark ONE letter for each question.
For example, if you think C is the right answer to the
question, mark your answer sheet like this:

0 A B C

Part 1

1 A B C
2 A B C
3 A B C
4 A B C
5 A B C

Part 2

6 A B C D E F G H
7 A B C D E F G H
8 A B C D E F G H
9 A B C D E F G H
10 A B C D E F G H

Part 3

11 A B C
12 A B C
13 A B C
14 A B C
15 A B C

For Parts 4 and 5:
Write your answers in the spaces next to the
numbers (16 to 25) like this:

0 example

Part 4

16
17
18
19
20

Do not
write here
1 16 0
1 17 0
1 18 0
1 19 0
1 20 0

Part 5

21
22
23
24
25

Do not
write here
1 21 0
1 22 0
1 23 0
1 24 0
1 25 0

KET L

DP314/088